THE CALL TO OBEY

THE CALL TO OBEY

by

MURDO EWEN MACDONALD

Minister of St. George's West Church, Edinburgh

HODDER AND STOUGHTON

PRINTED AND BOUND IN GREAT BRITAIN FOR
HODDER AND STOUGHTON LIMITED, ST. PAUL'S
HOUSE, WARWICK LANE, LONDON, E.C.4
BY C. TINLING AND CO., LIMITED, LIVERPOOL,
LONDON AND PRESCOT

CONTENTS

5

6   *Contents*

SECTION I

APOLOGETIC

INTRODUCTION

THE aim of this section is to present the Christian message to those inside and outside the Church who are sincerely puzzled by the apparent remoteness of theology. This means an inevitable tension between an intelligible approach to the modern mind on the one hand and an unequivocal declaration of the basic facts of the Christian faith on the other. There is a school of modern thought which regards the apologetic approach as an abject surrender to the pressures of secular culture. Admittedly, the very word "apologetic" has ambiguous associations, some of which carry a negative and defensive connotation, but that was never meant to be its role. The real aim of Christian apologetics is to shatter man's illusions, to strip him of his pretensions, to unmask his glib rationalisations, and to confront him in his spiritual nakedness with the totalitarian claims of the Gospel. The apologetic approach, however, is of little value unless it clears the way for a strong positive declaration. The preacher, while he must ever strive to understand a constantly changing world, must also proclaim the timeless truths of the Gospel and do justice to the "once and for all" nature of Christian revelation.

One or two of the sermons in this section appear without texts. I feel this is more honest than using a text merely as a pretext.

ARE WE DECEIVING
OURSELVES?

AUGUSTUS CAESAR was small of stature and all his life he had to struggle against poor health. But this delicate man made history and carved out for himself a career marked by glittering brilliance and a superb self-assurance. The explanation for his massive achievements, according to some biographers, can be traced back to a visit he paid as a young man to Theogenes, the celebrated astrologist. And when Theogenes read his horoscope, he fell on his face and worshipped him as a god. Augustus lived in a superstitious age that took astrology every bit as seriously as we take science nowadays. It never occurred to him that Theogenes might be wrong. From that moment he regarded himself as a man of destiny, and, harnessing himself to a powerful illusion, he swept all obstacles from his path.

This can happen not merely to individuals like Augustus Caesar, but to whole communities as well. Even in these latter days there is in Jamaica a tribe, called Ras Tifarians, who behave in a most eccentric manner. Living in a state of truculent isolation, they profess a weird form of religion. To them Haile Selassie is more than the emperor of Abyssinia—he is God incarnate. He is the long promised messiah come to deliver them out of poverty into a lush paradise situated somewhere in North Africa. Missionaries, educationists and psychologists have studied the beliefs of this strange sect, but all their efforts to disillusion them have proved futile. Every day they are seen wistfully scanning the horizon, looking for the ships that will transport them to the land of promise.

This, claim the sceptics, is precisely what religion is. On both the individual and collective level it is illusion pure and simple, a way of escape from the harsh, brutal actualities of our human existence, a headlong flight from reality. Nor is it altogether a foolish fantasy, they concede. Religion can be a useful illusion and can result in a number of beneficial by-products. It can uplift, inspire, encourage, and in the midst of stress it can induce a sense of poise and serenity. But, while this is so, religion is not related to any objective truth in the world outside our own inner feelings. From first to last it is a built-in emotional device, providing us with a measure of comfort in a cruel and unjust world.

Among doubting intellectuals this particular approach is the most popular and perhaps the most effective way of attacking religion. It sets out to demolish God, not by denying Him theologically, but by explaining Him away pyschologically. It launches its attack not on the surface where we can reply with logic and counter-argument, but under the threshold of personality where our motivating drives lie hidden in the depths of the unconscious. The case advanced by the sceptic may sound watertight and unanswerable, but examination proves that this is not so.

One answer is that if the illusion theory applies to

religion, it must of necessity apply to the whole of life. Even its severest critics must concede that religion is a major activity of the human spirit. Is it not arguable then that the other major activities of man—philosophy, psychology and science itself—may conceivably belong to the same category? Who knows but that man in all his researches is but a tool of some inscrutable life force that uses him for its own dark, enigmatic purpose. Some thinkers are honest enough to admit that we cannot stop at the place where we equate religion with illusion, that this very act opens up an abyss of scepticism stretching along the entire front of our human existence, into which not only religion but science itself tumbles out of sight.

There is another sense in which the illusion theory is ambivalent or double-edged. Religion may be what a modern writer has called it, "a research in comfort," but the same argument could be levelled against scepticism. Atheism can be a very comfortable philosophy. It not only reduces the intensity of moral conflict, but it renders the mystery of pain and suffering less poignant. The problem remains, it is true, but we are relieved of the agonising task of trying to harmonise the love of an all-powerful God with the evil in human nature and in history. And the atheist is in a position where he can nimbly side-step the charge of hypocrisy. If his creed is nil, he can go about accumulating credit for living better than his creed.

There is another fact which must embarrass the sceptic—the stubborn persistence of the need for religion. Not only is this a universal urge, but it has survived all the revolutionary upheavals and convulsive transitions of history. If it were fantasy and no more, surely mankind, that has shed so many superstitions, would have long since outgrown it. Yet Jung assures us that all the psychological problems that assail man today spring out of a profound religious need.

Still the problem remains. It is not possible to rebut the arguments of the sceptics by counter-arguments, however persuasively and trenchantly we may advance them. We must confront them with facts which cannot be gainsayed. Let us take then the whole bristling armoury of the familiar pyschological jargon—illusion, wishful thinking, escape mechanism—and examine it in the light of Christ's great prayer in Gethsemane, "Not my will, but thine be done".

This prayer teaches us that God calls us to a life not of self-indulgence but of self-renunciation. The only way in which the sceptic can seriously advance his "escape mechanism" theory is by shutting his eyes to the ruggedness of Christian character at its best. The epistle to the Hebrews supplies us with a roll of honour of those who suffered for their faith. "They were stoned, they were sawn asunder, were tempted, were slain with the sword." A curious mechanism, isn't it, which draws no clear distinction between comfort and martyrdom?

Self-renunciation, far from being exclusively a New Testament characteristic, has marked Christians throughout all ages, and is still an authentic badge of recognition. No Freudian theory of religion can explain away the courageous witness of men like Paul Schneider and Dietrich Bonhoeffer in terms of comfort alone, without distorting the evidence. In obedience to the Master whom they served, they rose above their own natural inclinations, and prayed, "Not my will, but thine be done". How then can we say that religion is nothing more than an escapist device, a drug by which we can endure the pain and face the challenges of life with a semblance of equanimity? The Cross and the countless numbers it has inspired is the answer to this sophisticated nonsense.

Again this prayer, "Not my will, but thine be done", teaches us that God strengthens us in hours of critical emergency. If religion is no better than a tranquilliser pill inducing a deceptive sense of well-being, it is difficult to see how it enables men to be steady and strong in times of cruel testing. There are times when doctors prescribe drugs, but they do so on the understanding that this is a temporary makeshift. At best, a drug is only a means which enables the person, sick in body or in mind, to recover his lost balance. And if religion is a drug, how do we explain the curious fact that its beneficial effects upon personality are so permanent? Is it not much more reasonable to suppose that a faith which enables men to cope triumphantly with crisis and calamity is rooted in reality itself?

In that remarkable book, *The Last Journal*, Captain Scott claims that the gruelling journey to and from the South Pole unerringly sifted out the strong from the weak, the invincible from the merely brave and admirable. And the man who stood head and shoulders above all the others was Edward Wilson. A devout

Christian, Scott saw him die of cold and starvation in a howling blizzard. It is difficult to imagine a more searching test of a man's character. Yet, according to the journal, Wilson died with a cheerful and hopeful equanimity. Surely here we see not the victim of an illusion, but a man who, fortified by a robust faith, had laid hold of the victory which overcomes the world.

Finally, this prayer, "Not my will, but thine be done", teaches us that God calls men not to escape from the world but to transform it. Jesus could have escaped if He had so wished. He need never have gone up to Jerusalem in the first place to expose Himself to the malignant fury of the Establishment. He could have avoided a head-on collision by saying nothing at all. Even on the eve of the Cross, while the Sanhedrin met to plot His destruction, all He needed to do was to mingle with the passover crowd and under cover of night to steal out of the city. But in Gethsemane Jesus sternly suppressed the temptation when in great agony He prayed, "Not my will, but thine be done". As we listen, we catch the accents not of stoical submission to the inevitable and the inescapable, but those of an ultimate confidence. Jesus did not run away from the Cross—He resolutely set His face in its direction and, in accepting it, He transformed the subsequent history of mankind. The Cross standing at the centre of Christianity, providing us with our most meaningful symbol, stands not for a cringing, comfort-loving escapism, but for a death-defying realism. That is why, after the lapse of centuries, millions of people can stand up and sing:

In the Cross of Christ I glory,
Towering o'er the wrecks of Time.
All the light of sacred story
Gathers round its head sublime.

The sceptics, brandishing their theory of illusion, would have us believe that Paul was trying to escape from the exacting demands of life when he suffered martyrdom in Rome upon the Appian way, that Martin Luther unwittingly was looking for comfort when, alone against the combined might of Church and State, he took his courageous stand and changed modern history, that the martyrs as they defied tyranny and went to the stake were, unknown to themselves, victims of the pleasure principle.

The sophisticated theory which claims that religion is a purely subjective phenomenon has been advanced by a number of formidable thinkers. We know they are wrong, not because we can expose their fallacies and detect flaws in their thinking, but because we have known people who have utterly confounded them. No theory, however brilliantly conceived and convincingly argued, can stand up to a personality who, instead of escaping from the world, actually transforms it. Jesus prayed His great prayer in Gethsemane nearly two thousand years ago, and, ever since, history has been different. This is not a comforting illusion we wrap round ourselves as we stand naked and shivering in the cold blast of the world's unbelief—it is a fact which the acids of modernity can never dissolve.

B

2

IS MORALITY ENOUGH?

THE Bolshevists, when they came to power in Russia, thought they had done away with what they contemptuously referred to as middle-class morality. In a few years, time-honoured restraints were forgotten and anarchy threatened to reign in the realm of individual conduct. If a man tired of his wife, he just left her and set up with the woman he fancied—no kind of contract, legal or otherwise, was necessary.

But this proved to be a passing phase. The more responsible leaders soon realised that morality was not just a bourgeois luxury which communism could afford to dispense with. It was necessary to hold society together. The initial reaction was violent, but within a single generation the pendulum began to swing back. It is surely one of the ironies of our time that Russia, parading an atheistic materialism, is far more puritanical about sex than the God-confessing democracies.

There is a prevailing theory, advanced by intellectuals and tacitly accepted by the masses, which claims that morality has nothing whatsoever to do with religion. Even if God were discredited as a myth, and the Church discarded as an archaic superstition, society, in the interests of sheer self-preservation, would need a measure of morality. After all, murderers must be tracked down and punished, thieves must be caught

and brought to the bar of justice. Our attitude to sex
may vary from one century to another, but there is no
race but has its own way of regulating it.

All this is undeniable. Society, if it is to maintain law
and order, needs a minimum level of morality. The
recognition of this fact seems, at first glance anyhow, to
play into the hands of the sceptic. If morality is auton-
omous, he argues, if it stands on its own legs without
the sanction of religion, why drag in the supernatural?
Is it not enough to appeal to commonsense and
enlightened self-interest?

There are those who are prepared to push the theory
even further. They claim that the agnostic is not only
capable of altruistic behaviour, but is often more
sensitive to suffering, and more responsive to the crying needs of his fellow-men than the large majority of
conventional Christians. This is the conviction that
throbs through Albert Camus's novel, *The Plague.*
Dr. Rieux, the hero of the book, nurses his own wife,
dying of T.B., with great tenderness, and when a deadly
bubonic plague broke out in his native town of Oran,
he is magnificently self-forgetful. He spent his strength
and risked his life every hour of the day for a people
who were not even grateful. Religion, argues Camus,
is not even a respectable luxury—a man can be a saint
without it.

To be sure we have all met sworn agnostics who have
challenged us to the depth of our being. Apparently
they can, with impunity, dispense with prayer and
worship and all the traditional creeds. We deceive
ourselves if we assume that they are hiding behind a

smoke screen of moral evasion. This, no doubt, is true of many, but it is by no means true of all sceptics. Disturbingly sincere, some of them are found in the very vanguard of the fight against poverty, disease and injustice. They present a challenge which the Church must take seriously and answer intelligently if she is to speak meaningfully to our age.

The Christian, while admitting that morality has a cohesive function in every society, claims that divorced from religion it tends to be no more than a matter of opinion. The philosopher, Thomas Hobbes, writing in the seventeenth century declared that there was no such thing as "Absolute goodness, considered without relation", thus paving the way for the ethical relativism which is so rampant in our midst today.

Hobbes and a select coterie of his celebrated contemporaries may have proved to their own satisfaction that morality was an entirely subjective affair, but the masses refused to take them seriously. Even those who flagrantly broke every commandment and committed every crime in the calendar never tried as we do to rationalise their behaviour on the ground that there were no fixed absolutes. Boswell was a rake. His conduct, especially where sex was concerned was more than loose and lascivious: it was, on occasions, swinish. But he did not glibly excuse himself, as so many literary celebrities today do, nor did he wax rich on pornography. Boswell, the sensualist, knew the meaning of guilt and suffered torments of conscience after every orgy, as his recently published diaries show.

The same, even to a greater extent, was true of the

Victorian age. It produced a crop of celebrated agnostics who were at the same time pillars of moral rectitude. John Morley, the first biographer of Gladstone, John Stuart Mill, Herbert Spencer and George Eliot, the novelist, were all people of this stamp. They questioned the existence of God, but it never occurred to them to question the existence of absolute moral imperatives that were independent of all but human opinion.

This is no longer the case. Our age is perhaps characterised by its ethical relativism more than by anything else. Philosophers expound it, writers romanticise it, psychologists take it for granted and it is becoming part of the mental outfit of the ordinary man. He slides out from under every challenge, with the glib retort that what is right for you is not necessarily right for him. It depends on circumstances, on environment, on heredity, and a whole host of complex factors over which he has no control. No wonder confusion abounds. No wonder crime and juvenile delinquency are rampant. No wonder countries are at sixes and sevens politically. If there are no absolute imperatives, it means that what Russia likes is morally right for Russia, and what America likes is morally right for America, with Britain playing the same relativistic game, somewhere in between. Ethical relativism is the archenemy of integration of all levels of our existence.

The Christian is also prepared to claim that morality divorced from religion is not self-sustaining. The Old Testament makes it plain that the roots of morality and religion are inextricably intertwined. Isaiah's mystical experience in the temple expressed itself in a heightened sense of individual and social morality. "Holy, holy, holy is the Lord God of hosts," cried the prophet, and the inexorable logic follows, "Woe is me for I am undone because I am a man of unclean lips, and I dwell in the midst of a people of unclean lips." Micah, another prophet with an intense awareness of God's unquestioned sovereignty, reminds us of the indissoluble marriage that must ever exist between creed and conduct. "What doth the Lord require of thee, but to do justly, and to love mercy and to walk humbly with thy God." And the psalmist will not countenance any separation: "The sacrifices of God are a broken spirit: a broken and a contrite heart, O God thou wilt not despise."

The New Testament is even more explicit. This book may not be a compendium of moral maxims, an ethical highway code, giving specific instructions for every possible contingency, but it does say, "By their fruits ye shall know them". The teaching of Jesus was no doubt non-legislative, but when He preached He expected a response that issued in definite action— "And every one that heareth these sayings of mine, and doeth them not, shall be likened unto a foolish man which built his house upon the sand." And John, interpretating his Master's mind, wrote; "He that loveth not, knoweth not God, for God is love." The New Testament turns a stern face to the assumption we so glibly make that belief can be divorced from behaviour.

The truth is that morality cannot operate indefinitely under its own momentum. Thomas Huxley is often cited as an example of a man who was irreligious, yet lived an exemplary life, morally. No doubt he was a good man, but the question we must ask is whether he succeeded in transmitting his moral principles to the next generation and the next after. He did not. He was drawing on an inherited, but fast-dwindling, moral capital. This becomes clear if we read the searing confession of his grandson, Aldous, in his book *Ends and Means*. There Aldous Huxley argues that a creedless morality is neither self-sustaining nor self-perpetuating. It inevitably peters out, leaving behind it a legacy of desolating emptiness and impotent despair.

The whole civilised world was profoundly shocked by the Nazi savagery, practised with all the sadistic refinements of modern science. But why should this be? Discerning minds could foresee the camps of Belsen and Buchenwald a generation or two before Eichmann built his gas chambers and elaborated his satanic butcheries. It was the inevitable consequence of the attempt not only to discredit Christianity, but also to disown all religion.

And on the level of individual behaviour, the same inexorable law operates. According to writers like C. E. M. Joad and Gerald Heard, there has been a catastrophic slump in private morals since 1900. But again, why be surprised? Victorian sceptics could snap their fingers at God, and go on behaving themselves tolerably well, but not their grandchildren. After all, as John Baillie puts it, "A railway engine does not stop as soon as the driver shuts off the steam, nor does a turnip wither and die the moment it is pulled out of Mother

Earth." No! but the thing to note is that in time the locomotive will come to a dead stop and the turnip will inevitably shrivel up. Such is the fate of any system of morality which is not firmly rooted in the soil of religion.

Finally, the Christian asserts that morality divorced from religion lacks power. The prophets of the cult of decency can be exasperatingly smug. Apart from the fact that the Christian faith is something infinitely more dynamic than decency, they have no liberating gospel for a man who has given up the moral struggle and has acquiesced in defeat. They have no hope to hold out to the chronic alcoholic, the drug addict, the helpless victim of devouring and demonic passions. Baron von Munchhausen, the celebrated liar, once fell into a bog. When he had sunk up to the neck and the situation looked desperate, he worked the miracle by the simple expedient of grabbing his hair and pulling himself out. The humanist recipes for our moral predicaments sound equally absurd if not quite so funny.

Modern ingenuity can catapult men into outer space and bring them back safely to earth, and soon it may send them to land on other planets. But there is one thing it cannot do—it cannot effect the miracle of regeneration. Modern man is brilliant and versatile, but there are limits to his ingenuity. Not the labour of his hands, not the cleverness of his brain, not the concentration of his will, can raise to newness of life someone who is dead in "trespasses and sins".

Morality is strong in principle but weak in power.

It tells us what we ought to do, but does not enable us to translate aspiration into actuality. It bludgeons us with categorical imperatives till we find ourselves dazed and teetering over a precipice of absolute despair. This is what happened to men like Paul and Augustine and Luther. They had powerful minds and tenacious wills, but the more they struggled against their own tumultuous passions, the more they were overwhelmed by them. What we most desperately need is not an ideal to aim at, but power "to stand in the evil day, and having done all, to stand". It is the unanimous testimony of mystics and martyrs, of men of deep spiritual discernment, and of countless multitudes of ordinary people, that Jesus Christ succeeds where all human therapy fails.

In Walter Scott's novel, *Old Mortality*, the blind Covenanter woman says, "Mony a hungry, starving creature, when he sits down on a Sunday forenoon to get something that might warm him to his great work, has a dry clatter of morality down about his lugs." This is not what we mean by the Christian message. The New Testament is not a book on moral philosophy, nor is it a collection of vague ethical principles. From beginning to end it proclaims a God who is able to bind up the broken-hearted, to set the captives free, and to lead those who sit in darkness into His own marvellous light. Jesus Christ did not come into the world either to edify or to exhort—He came to save us from our sins, He "is the power of God unto salvation to every one that believeth".

3

MYSTERY AND KNOWLEDGE

"For now we see through a glass darkly."

I Corinthians 13, 12

AT the risk of oversimplifying complexities which defy a simple straightforward analysis, we could claim that in the main the enemies of the Christian religion can be divided into two classes. The first category is comprised of those who regard mystery as a confession of ignorance and nothing else. They believe that no phenomenon, however strange and mysterious it may appear to us, is to be explained in terms of the supernatural. If there is any phenomenon which seems to defy a natural explanation, we must wait till our conception of cause and effect has become enlarged. And if there is a phenomenon which, even theoretically, eludes a causal explanation, such as the indeterminate behaviour of the atom, God is absolutely ruled out. "The history of scientific advance," writes J. D. Bernal, "has shown us clearly that any appeal to divine purpose or any supernatural agency to explain any phenomenon is in fact only a concealed confession of ignorance."

The protagonists of this view may be found under a variety of labels. Some may choose to call themselves agnostics, others militant atheists, others still, scientific or philosophical humanists; but whatever the particular emphasis, they are one in assuming that one day all mystery will be transmuted into knowledge. Given time, science will provide an adequate explanation for all things under, and including, the sun.

The second category is made up of those who believe in the supernatural, yet tend to undermine religion by parading an orthodoxy which is too narrow. Not for a moment would they claim that our existence here is self-explanatory, but their answers to the enigmas that haunt us are too facile. There are some people who are deceived and even comforted by this kind of confidence, but there are others who know that life as they have known and experienced it plays sheer havoc with systems of thought that are too sharply defined. There is a kind of theological dogmatism that does more damage to religion than the most truculent brand of atheism. By erring on the side of over-confidence, it is insensitive to mystery and clouds the meaning of Christian certitude.

An authentic Christian faith is very different. It avoids on the one hand the intellectual smugness of the humanist, and on the other the strident assertiveness of the dogmatist. Conscious of the fragmentariness of all knowledge, it comes to terms with the inevitable tension that must exist between mystery and knowledge. Who in the entire history of Christianity possessed a stronger sense of certitude than the apostle Paul? Here is his own testimony: "For I am persuaded that neither death, nor life, nor angels, nor principalities, nor powers, nor things present, nor things to come, nor height, nor depth, nor any other creature, shall be able to separate us from the love of God, which is in Christ Jesus our Lord." Paul was gloriously sure, but at the same time he was conscious of the fact that our knowledge was a broken and partial thing and that our divinings of truth were shrouded in deepest mystery. This is the apostolic confession encapsuled in the memorable words, "Now we see through a glass darkly". Is this observation no more than a striking metaphor, or is it an authentic description of life as we have actually experienced it?

We see through a glass darkly when we contemplate the mystery of the universe itself. There is a common belief held with considerable tenacity, even by educated people, that the more science there is, the less mystery is left. Because it has elucidated so many of our enigmas and scattered so many of our superstitions, it is assumed that in time it will explain everything including God Himself.

> "God is a proposition
> And we that prove Him are His priests, His chosen,
> From bare hypotheses
> Of strata and wind, of stars and tide, watch me
> Construct His Universe.
> Last week I measured the Light, His little finger,
> The rest is a matter of time."

The paradox, however, is that science, far from diminishing, has immeasurably increased, the mystery of the universe. The world which Copernicus scanned was in all conscience baffling enough, but what of the world disclosed to us by modern astronomy? Consider the innumerable planets, the whirling nebulae, the millions of superheated suns, the unfathomable abysses of empty space, its unthinkable distances measured in light years, and if that doesn't induce humility, nothing can. The truth is that the universe of Fred Hoyle is a thousand times more mysterious than that of Isaac Newton.

We also see through a glass darkly when we contemplate the mystery of evil. The cancer cell, the tapeworm and the typhoid bacillus cannot be ascribed to man's misuse of his free will. He cannot be blamed for the widespread devastation they cause. And though he is responsible for many of his moral lapses, it is also true that he was born with a built-in bias in his nature towards sin. We have all experienced the schizophrenic split which Paul so succinctly describes, "The good that I would, I do not, and the evil that I would not, that I do."

Those who would explain away evil in terms of ignorance or economic injustice are guilty of unpardonable shallowness. These trite and twittering platitudes are an offence to anyone who has experienced the full sadistic fury of man's inhumanity to man. Those who, like Mary Baker Eddy, would describe evil as the absence of the good are denying its objective reality and are guilty of a cruel and monstrous absurdity. Those who, like Margaret Knight the humanist, would advance an aesthetic explanation are really tinkering with the problem. To say that pain is as essential to life as minor discords are to a major musical composition, contributing to the meaning and balance of the whole, is tantamount to denying the existence of evil. It is only an appearance not a reality.

The Christian, on the other hand, affirms the reality of evil. It is not an illusion or an appearance or even a discord; it is a brute fact of our existence. Nor does he try to prevaricate by taking total refuge in mystery. Mystery indeed there is, but it is mystery which is shot through and through with meaning. The Cross on which Jesus died is the symbol both of the evil in the world and of the divine purpose which runs through it.

Still further we see through a glass darkly when we contemplate the mystery of man himself. "What is man?" asked the psalmist, posing one of the most fundamental questions that has ever been put. One answer is that man is a chemical mixture of atoms and molecules—the fundamental elements of the universe—what the Bible means when it claims that man was formed from dust. Another answer is that man is an animal, and who would deny that there are striking similarities and that we have much in common? But man is more than the stuff the stars are made of, more than the built-in collection of instincts which drive animals to suckle their young and to perpetuate their kind; he has something of the divine in his make-up. That is what the Bible means when it says, "So God created man in his own image". It is this quality which enables man to survey the ages and to stand outside his own predicament. He may experience anxiety, but he is also able to address himself and ask, "Why art thou cast down, O my soul?" Man, an amphibious creature, a citizen of two worlds, an irreconcilable mixture of devil and angel, will ever remain an enigma to himself.

"We see through a glass darkly," confesses the Apostle who looked upon the Christian faith as a divine revelation which remained a mystery in its very revelation. We may well ask how we can approach the vastness of the mystery environing us, without forgetting the fragmentariness of our knowledge; yet without falling into the pit of an abject and despairing attitude towards it. In what way can we obtain clear and unmistakable intimations of what in full scope transcends our reason and eludes our grasp. We only know in part and there is no use pretending otherwise.

> Our knowledge is a torch of smoky pine
> That lights the pathway but one step ahead
> Across a void of mystery and dread.

This is true, but the fact remains that we do see, and the light which God has given us in Jesus Christ is as much as we need to know and more than we are likely to use. What then are the instruments, if any, at the Christian's disposal which enable him not only to approach mystery with some degree of confidence but also in a measure to pierce through it? Towards the end of this tremendous chapter, Paul mentions them by name.

The first is faith. Whenever the word is mentioned, the modern mind instinctively recoils from it as if this way of looking at things was a medieval legacy not yet relegated to oblivion. But when Christians talk of faith, they mean by it not something which is contrary to knowledge, but something which makes knowledge possible. Science, which lays such a strong emphasis on verification, is itself built on a colossal act of faith. It is based on a number of assumptions which cannot be proved. It assumes, among other things, that the universe is rational and that our mind—itself a mystery—is capable of interpreting it correctly.

For the Christian, however, faith is not a set of universal axioms, but a personal relationship with the God who revealed His innermost nature to us in Jesus Christ. The scientist in all his explorations and experiments proceeds on the basis of the trustworthiness of the universe. The Christian orders his life and makes his witness in a perplexing world, on the basis of the trustworthiness of Jesus Christ.

The second instrument with which Christians can penetrate the veil of mystery is hope. As long as man has hope, life may buffet him but it will never break him. He may be perplexed, but he is not in despair, cast down but not destroyed. But it must be Christian hope, not the vague sentimental optimism of Mr. Micawber in *David Copperfield*. It is when Christian hope goes, leaving a desolating emptiness, that intelligent people are prone to take an overdose of sleeping tablets and leave sad little notes behind.

The belief in the Life Everlasting stands at the very heart of the New Testament, but while this is so, the New Testament is strangely reticent about the exact nature of the hereafter. We look in vain for the detailed knowledge of post-mortem existence so dear to the heart of the students of psychic research. It contents itself with preaching the Christian hope. Significantly, Paul, after acknowledging that we only see through a glass darkly, goes on to affirm that one day we shall see face to face. And Peter, scorning argument, makes a triumphant affirmation—"Blessed be the God and Father of our Lord Jesus Christ, which according to his abundant mercy hath begotten us again unto a lively hope by the resurrection of Jesus Christ from the dead." Hope is but another name for faith with its face turned towards the future.

The third is love. We can get to know the properties of radium by suitable laboratory tests. We can get to know what the moon is made of by building bigger rockets and space capsules and landing someone there. We can get to know a foreign language by studying its syntax and amassing its vocabulary. But we cannot get to know a person except by loving him, and there is no exception to this rule. That is why personal relationship is so different from every other kind of relationship, and why the New Testament makes love absolutely central: "He that loveth not, knoweth not God, for God is love." God is not an abstract first cause or a cosmic absolute, but a Person who can only be known through love. And love means an attitude of goodwill towards all men, even towards those who despise and persecute us. The New Testament recognises no distinction between loving God and loving our neighbour. John, in his epistle, is disturbingly explicit on this point: "He that hateth his brother is in darkness and walketh in darkness."

c

The Christian, standing on the edge of vast mysteries about which he knows not yet all the answers, is only sure of Christ. He walks in confidence, though not yet with full knowledge, believing that there will come a day when the meaning shall be made plain and the mystery shall be revealed—"And now abideth faith, hope, love, these three, but the greatest of these is love."

4

THE RETICENCE OF GOD

"But we have this treasure in earthen vessels, that the excellency of the power may be of God, and not of us."

II Corinthians 4, 7.

In ancient Israel, banks were non-existent, so a common way of securing wealth was to change it into gold, place it in an earthenware jar and bury it deep in the earth. Sometimes it happened that the owner died or that in war he was taken prisoner and no one knew where the money was hid. And so, hundreds, perhaps thousands of years later, a farmer's plough shattered the fragile casing and gold coins would pour out. Paul, writing to Corinth, a wealthy sea-port preoccupied with merchandise and trade, refers to this traditional practice to drive home an important truth—the contrast between the gift of faith and the container which holds it. "We have this treasure in earthen vessels, that the excellency of the power may be of God, and not of us."

We could take this insight of Paul and apply it to the Bible. Many of us have, no doubt, heard of the Dead Sea Scrolls, the discovery which, a few years ago, threw the world of archaeology and Biblical scholarship into a frenzy of excitement. It began with a Bedouin shepherd throwing a stone into a cave and hearing a sound like that of breaking crockery. Next day, with a companion, he entered the cave and found tall earthenware jars containing packages wrapped in linen and coated with pitch. Inside they discovered manuscripts written in parallel columns which they tried to sell in Jerusalem for twenty pounds, little dreaming that they had in their possession one of the most valuable documents ever unearthed by man.

My purpose in relating this story is to draw attention to a myth which has gathered round the Bible—the myth of a magical and mechanical infallibility. Some people believe that the Bible, as we have it, was not written by men, but by God himself. He took, as it were the wrists of the various authors and decreed that every chapter, every sentence, every word was infallible. Call this what you will, verbal inspiration, fundamentalism, inerrancy of scripture, but it is a disastrous attitude in an age when religion is fighting for its life, when we need all the guidance and spiritual resources the Bible can offer us. At Waterloo, Wellington defeated Napoleon by taking up a strong position where he could deploy his forces to advantage, and it is imperative that Christians do battle with the enemies of the faith from a position of strength, not from one which has become indefensible.

The thing we have to admit is that in scripture God spoke through fallible men. If any part of the Bible bears upon it the authentic divine imprint, it is surely the ten commandments. Yet we know that the man who was inspired by God to write, "Thou shalt not kill", was himself a murderer. If I had been Moses, I would have seen to it that the ugly story of the killing of the Egyptian was expunged from Holy Writ. Yet there it stands that we may see Moses not merely as the wise law-giver, but also as a man of like passions as ourselves. His past is honestly portrayed in order that we may get a passing glimpse of the miracles of character the grace of God can effect.

But if we repudiate the mechanical verbal infallibility of scripture, how can we proclaim it convincingly as the Word of God? The answer surely is that the attitude to the Bible, I am now advocating, adds to rather than subtracts from its authority. We give the Bible a central place in our worship not because we regard it as great literature but because we regard it as the Word of God. We accord it an honour we give no other book, not because we believe it to be the story of man's search for God, but because we believe it to be the story of the divine initiative—of the God who tirelessly pursues men till at the end their seeking is turned to finding.

How can we believe the Bible is the Word of God when some of the men who wrote it were so very human and so distressingly fallible? Emil Brunner, the great modern theologian, offers us a modern analogy by way of answering this question. If we buy a gramophone record, say of Caruso, we are assured that we will have no difficulty in recognising the great singer's voice. It goes without question that this is true. But while listening to Caruso's voice, we are aware of other discordant noises, caused by flaws in the disc and by the scratching of a far from perfect needle. Yet we must not become impatient with either disc or needle, for it is only by means of them that the voice we want to hear becomes audible. And so it is with the Bible. Moses and Peter and John may not be perfect instruments but it is through them that we hear God speak. Only a fool will concentrate on the incidental noises and miss the authentic voice. It is possible for Christians to be thoroughly modern and at the same time accept the authority of the Bible. Distortions and distracting sounds may be there, but they do not muffle the voice of God which speaks to us all the way from Genesis to Revelation. "We have this treasure in earthen vessels, that the excellency of the power may be of God, and not of us."

Again, we could take this insight of Paul and apply it to the Church. Those of us who love the Church know the meaning of shame. We shudder at what the world thinks of our divisions, our bourgeois complacency, our bungling sectarian ineptitude. Is this indeed the instrument of God's will in history, the vehicle of His invincible purpose, the very Body of Christ on earth? In his book, *The Recovery of Belief*, C. E. M. Joad wrote, "No sin in the calendar has been committed more flagrantly and more continuously than by the professed servants and ministers of the Church. Nevertheless, the Church has survived the excesses of its ministers and members. How, one is tempted to wonder, could it have done so unless God Himself kept it alive?"

Significantly, the first commandment is "Thou shalt have no other gods before me". This is so because the sin the Jews most frequently succumbed to was idolatry

—the bowing of the knee to false gods, the exalting of the perishable above the permanent, the acceptance of error and the rejection of truth. And isn't idolatry in all its multitudinous expressions the characteristic sin of the twentieth century too? Nowhere is it more evident than in our arrogant ecclesiastical claims in which we tend to equate the purely temporal with the eternal.

The Roman Catholic Church, maintaining as it does that it is the one and only Church, is guilty of idolatry. The Protestant Church is also guilty of idolatry in that it, or at least sections of it, imagine the Reformation is complete, or even that it can ever be completed this side of time. The year when we celebrated the fourth centenary of the Reformation in Scotland happened also to be the year when the question of the admission of women to the eldership was discussed by our Presbyteries. And in Edinburgh I heard leaders of the Church stand up and, in shocked tones, exclaim, "Women elders! What would John Knox say?" This was their way of celebrating the Reformation—a grim determination to stifle change and resist every attempt to reform.

The Christian ideal for the Church is ultimate unity. On the eve of the Cross, Jesus prayed that the Church might be one, and Paul describes the Church as the Body of Christ—"the fullness of Him that filleth all in all;" which means, if it means anything, that our aim is eventual unity between the Roman and Protestant Churches. At the moment this seems impossible, but as a preliminary step we must rid ourselves of muddle-headed ambiguities, encouraged as they undoubtedly are by ecumenical wistfulness. We must never forget that the Roman and Protestant Churches have much in common. They worship the one God, confess the same Christ as Lord, and believe in the Life Everlasting, but it is on the doctrine of the Church that they come into head-on collision. Let it be said that on the administrative and pastoral levels we have much to learn from Roman Catholicism, and this we must acknowledge with humility. But while this is so, we must know wherein we differ. There can be no progress towards ultimate unity till we see the thing that really separates us standing out in all its unambiguous, disconcerting and disturbing sharpness.

The Roman Catholic Church, while it admits it is a community of sinners, will not admit it is a sinful community. On the contrary, it claims that, in the basic sense, it is irreformable and that its dogmas are infallible. The Protestant Church, on the other hand, at its best acknowledges that it is not merely a community of sinners, but that it is also a sinful community. This is the inner nerve of our difference and there is no hope of reconciliation till we arrive at an understanding on this basic issue.

The danger inherent in Protestant sectarianism is the assumption that the treasure of faith can be had without the earthenware vessels (of ecclesiastical systems)—that the vessels are not necessary. The danger inherent in Roman Catholicism is that of equating the earthen vessels with the treasure itself, of asserting that the vessels of their particular system are more than earthen. What we must grasp is that all ecclesiastical systems are no more than earthen vessels, and as such are liable to be broken and smashed. The important thing is the treasure contained within them. Yes, Paul's words apply to the Church, "We have this treasure in earthen vessels that the excellency of the power may be of God and not of us."

Finally, we could take this insight of Paul and apply it to personality. Of all forms of attack against religion, the psychological is by far the most devastating. It launches its assault not by denying God or discrediting the Church, but by explaining away personal faith in terms of fantasy, illusion and wishful thinking. Freud and his followers draw our attention to man's animal inheritance. The unconscious which they have unmasked is a seething cauldron of repressed lusts, selfish impulses and anti-social habits, and God is just a cosmic chloroform mask into which we stick our faces when we are lonely and afraid.

At the Edinburgh Festival I saw John Osborne's *Martin Luther*. It is a powerful play which in places shows flashes of sympathetic insight and a fine sense of theatre. This is so, but the figure that finally emerges, though we are compelled to admire his courage, his integrity, his robust masculinity, and to share in his agony, is not the Luther we were traditionally taught to revere. We get the impression that the anguish leading up to his conversion is another name for repressed guilt, which could be dispelled by modern therapeutic methods, and that his revolt has its roots in the peculiar relationship between himself and an authoritarian strong-willed father, issuing in an avowed antagonism against a totalitarian Church.

Our answer to the Freudians in general, and to John Osborne in particular, is that there may be a great deal of truth in their analysis; but that it is by no means the whole truth. After all, the Christian doctrine of man makes no effort to whitewash personality. It claims that man is a sinner full of wickedness and selfishness and self-deception, and that even the purest of the saints are of the earth earthy. But it also claims that somewhere in the common clay of our nature there lurks a divine spark—a capacity for God, an undying kinship with Christ, and therefore miracles in the realm of character are possible.

This then is our strategy as we cross swords with the critics of the Christian faith. We fight them not on the ground chosen by them towards which they are for ever trying to lure us, but on the kind of ground we can defend with intelligence and integrity. We are careful not to invest the Bible with the wrong kind of infallibility or the Church with a spurious perfectionism, or personality with virtues that do not rightly belong to it. That is the surest way to court humiliation and defeat. Our confidence springs from the fact that if history is any guide, God has used men full of faults and infirmities to further and fulfil His own purpose in the world. We offer Him not our unified strength but our conflicts, our inner tensions, our inarticulate longings, and out of this unprepossessing material He works His miracles. To this divine strategy, which turns liabilities into assets and weakness into strength, evil has no answer. This is the victory that overcometh the world. 'We have this treasure in earthen vessels that the excellency of the power may be of God and not of us."

5

CAN WE KNOW GOD?

In T. S. Eliot's play, *The Cocktail Party*, Reilly, whose utterances carry the main message of the author, says:

> There is another way, if you have the courage.
> The first I could describe in familiar terms
> Because you have seen it, as we all have seen it
> Illustrated, more or less, in the lives of those about us.
> The second is unknown and so requires faith.
> The kind of faith that issues from despair.
> The destination cannot be described.
> You will know very little till you get there
> You will journey blind. But the way leads towards possession
> Of what you have sought for in the wrong place.

There the poet is expressing in moving language what many people passionately believe. God is not unknowable. He can be experienced, provided the seeker is prepared to submit himself to the rigorous discipline which even the least ambitious branch of secular knowledge so sternly demands. It goes without saying, of course, that seeking is a form of finding, that unless God himself has already taken the initiative no amount of searching on our part ever avails. The tormented Pascal, who searched so long and so agonisingly, at length heard a voice which said to him "Thou wouldst not then be seeking me had'st thou not already found me".

Seeking and Finding, James Reid
Jeremiah 29:13

All this is undeniably true. Still the puzzling fact remains that the saints are triumphantly certain, that others are reasonably sure, but that the majority are still in the realm of opinion. There are many sincere agnostics known to myself who want to believe in God. They have peered into the abyss of meaninglessness towards which unbelief willy-nilly pushes us, but the word, God, is no more than a word, carrying with it a few, vague, transient feelings which mean nothing at all in the context of terrible world-shaking events.

Our deepest and most desperate need today is a central conviction about God. Opinions we have in plenty, but conviction, that is what we secretly long for, yet never seem to possess. Few of us are militant atheists crying like the fool in the psalms, "There is no God". Most of us feel that this mysterious universe did not create and organise itself any more than a Beethoven symphony came fortuitously together. With Matthew Arnold we believe that behind the contradictions of history there is "something, not ourselves, that makes for righteousness". But that is as far as we ever get. God is not a certainty, but a half-formed, nebulous theory, floating about in the hinterland of our thinking.

We must reject the theory that some men are born with the mystic consciousness and others are born without it, and that the latter can never know God. The truth is that deep down below the threshold of our ordinary consciousness there is a dim, smothered awareness of the Divine, which in the great mystic blazes in the full light of conscious recognition. A man may call himself an agnostic or an atheist, but it does not follow that he is irreligious. What he has may only amount to an unclothed feeling, unclothed with any creed or symbol, inarticulate and formless.

According to the Bible and the great experts of the spiritual life, all men if they so wish can cross the boundary-line which separates opinion from conviction. Provided they fulfil certain conditions, they can lay hold of the inner assurance which will enable them to cry with the psalmist, "O God thou art my God". Let this then be the theme of our sermon—the leap from outer conformity to inner conviction, from traditional acquiescence to personal apprehension.

In grappling with the problem let us consider first, *the place of reason in religion.* Reason has always played a prominent part in religion and must continue to do so. Jesus Himself commanded us to love God with our minds. Wherever and whenever faith and reason have become divorced from one another, religion has, in the course of time, degenerated into superstition. This has happened in Abyssinia and in some parts of South America—hence the clamant need for theology. To be sure, theology itself will not create a living faith in any man, but it fulfils an important function in relating faith to the rest of human knowledge and in interpreting its meaning for us in the kind of world we live in.

There are those, of course, who dismiss revelation as a theological red-herring, claiming that if there is a God, reason and reason alone should supply us with a knowledge of His existence. They would have us make

God an object of rational enquiry. They would have us reduce Him to the level of every other question that stimulates human curiosity. They would have us seeking Him the way men have sought radium and penicillin and the cure for malaria. All such efforts are in the end doomed to disappointment for a very simple reason. If God could be discovered by the method of scientific enquiry, He would cease to be the God of the Bible, the ground and the meaning of our human existence.

In the course of my ministry, many people have come to me saying, "We have given up the search for God. We feel that if men of the intelligence of George Bernard Shaw and Bertrand Russell have looked for Him and have not found Him, we don't have much of a chance." This argument rests on the fallacy that reason by itself can unravel ultimate mystery and can generate the inner sense of certainty which characterises the religious man. There are five classical proofs of the existence of God, and though no doubt they serve a useful purpose in clarifying our thinking, they are powerless to create inner conviction.

Perhaps, far from lamenting this, we should actually rejoice and be glad. After all, if reason by itself could lead us to God, most of us would have little or no chance. The brilliant, and especially the geniuses, would have an enormous advantage over the rank and file of humanity, and the supreme discovery would be the exclusive property of an intellectually *élite* class. Surely such a possibility plays sheer havoc with the basic presuppositions of the Christian faith which assert that the way to God is open to all, however simple and untutored they may be. Surely, we can safely assume that the key which opens up for us the ultimate mystery must be such as to be within the reach of all the children of men.

Or again consider *the place of authority in religion.* In his *Spiritual Exercises*, Ignatius Loyola writes, "We ought always to be ready to believe that what seems to us white, is black, if the Church so defines it." I doubt if any of us brought up to the Protestant tradition could conceivably subscribe to such a sentiment. Cardinal Newman possessed a profoundly religious soul, coupled with an essentially sceptical intelligence. This tension he resolved by yielding unquestioning obedience to the Mother Church, but this solution is barred to most of us. Let this be said, however, some Roman Catholics who rest on the authority of a so-called infallible Church are more contented and more free from psychological disorder than many Protestants who, in relinquishing the traditional faith, have become nervous. They have emancipated themselves from ecclesiastical and authoritarian control, but they are aware of a dangerous vacuum within.

Is there a sense in which Protestants can appeal to authority without investing the institutional Church with a dubious infallibility? I am sure there is. The Christian in all humility must admit that individual experience, even at its best, is but fragmentary and incomplete and that he is aware of immense vistas of truth stretching far out beyond his own reach. William James, the famous psychologist, filled up a questionnaire which among other queries asked, "Is God very real to you? Do you feel that you have experienced His presence?" Then followed the question, "If you have had no such experience, do you accept the testimony of others who claim they have felt God's presence directly?" To which James replies—"Yes. The whole line of testimony on this point is so strong that I am unable to pooh-pooh it away."

We have only to read our Bible, our hymn books or the biographies of saints and mystics to discover that personal conviction is not an isolated phenomenon, but rather one link in a long chain of evidence stretching back across the ages. Is this unanimity of belief, this unbroken chain of witness, to be dismissed then as the confused babblings of deluded cranks? Surely not! So convincing is it in its cumulative effect, that with William James we are forced to say, "We are unable to pooh-pooh it away".

Finally consider *the place of obedience in religion.* In the Bible faith and obedience are inseparable, and Jesus goes out of His way to stress this indissoluble relationship. Again and again we hear the same note break forth, "I thank Thee O Father, because Thou hast hid these things from the wise and prudent, and hast revealed them unto babes." And again, "Blessed are the pure in heart, for they shall see God." And still again, in the gospel of John, "If any man will do His will, he shall know of the doctrine whether it be of God." Nowhere does Jesus promise the vision of God to the smooth or to the clever. This is the reward given to the children of obedience. *"The Call to Obey"*

D

Some time ago, I read a book called *The Prof.* which is a personal memoir of the late Lord Cherwell, one time Professor of Physics at Oxford University and scientific adviser to Winston Churchill during the last war. Portrayed as he was, by one of his own close friends, I found the Prof. a singularly unattractive character. Arrogant, self-opinionated, socially ruthless, he was a snob of snobs—one of those figures we still tolerate and even revere in our caste-ridden society. Yet, despite my repulsion, I found myself profoundly challenged by the Prof. and especially by something he did during the First War. At that time, any pilot who got himself in a spin, crashed and was lost with the aeroplane. The Prof. studied this problem and managed to convert the aerodynamics of a spinning dive into a mathematical formula, and argued that if a pilot were to act in a certain way, he could correct the spin. The commandant of the aerodrome was interested in the theory, but felt he could not reasonably expect any pilot to put it to the test on the strength of a mere formula jotted down on a piece of paper. The Prof. however, came forward and said, "Teach me to fly and I will prove to you that the theory is true." Within three weeks of qualifying, he flew up alone to a great height, deliberately put himself into a spinning dive and demonstrated that the formula worked. Not content with that, he insisted on going up again and showed that it also worked in an anti-clockwise direction.

This is as good an example as I know of the meaning of the Christian faith. We have the formula in our hands, the doctrines hammered out by the seers and thinkers of the past, and it is up to us, to demonstrate to ourselves and to others, that this thing works.

But someone may reasonably protest that to talk of Christian obedience to an unbeliever is absurd, if not indeed impertinent. How can we obey a God whose existence we are inclined to doubt? The answer is that there is a place where we can begin. Whether we believe in God or not, we are conscious of certain moral demands it is not possible to evade. The philosopher, Kant, calls this awareness "the categorical imperative" —a cumbersome phrase perhaps, but one which makes sense to us all. We have been given a certain amount of light and we are commanded to follow that light wherever it leads us. If someone retorts that he lacks the will to respond, the Bible answers that, provided he is prepared to make the leap, God's grace is sufficient for him and the divine strength is made perfect in human weakness.

SECTION II

EXPOSITORY

1 The parable of the unjust steward
2 The parable of the tares
3 The parable of the good samaritan
4 The parable of the talents
5 The parable of the leaven

INTRODUCTION

IF the Bible is the written witness of God's revelation of Himself and of His dealings with men, there is a sense in which all preaching must be expository. Because this is so, the choice of sermons included under this section is to some extent arbitrary. I have deliberately selected the parables on the ground that within their compass we get the kernel of Christ's teaching on God, man and Himself.

There is a sense in which the parables of Jesus lend themselves to expository preaching more readily than the rest of His teaching. Three things are responsible for this. The first is the narrative form which has the practical advantage of supplying the preacher with a ready-made framework. The second is the unavoidable question: What did Jesus, in the context of His own ministry, intend to convey by this story? The third is also in the nature of a question: How did the early Church interpret this story and apply it to its own life? (This kind of problem is illustrated by the four different interpretations offered by the Evangelist for the parable of the unjust steward.) Even if a preacher fails in applying the parable to his own world, in asking these questions, he is at least grappling with the issue raised by the text.

In these five sermons I would like to acknowledge my indebtedness to Professor Joachim Jeremias, whose book, *The Parables of Jesus*, revolutionised my whole attitude to them. Another book I found helpful is Professor A. M. Hunter's *Introduction to the Parables*.

THE PARABLE OF
THE UNJUST STEWARD

ST. LUKE 16, 1–13

THIS is not an anaemic allegory with an ambiguous moral, but a story based on an actual happening, known to Jesus personally, or related to him on good authority. It records the behaviour of a factor who was discovered in the process of double-crossing his master. Called to account, he retrieved what looked like an impossible situation by a most ingenious plan. He falsified the entries in the book, and by debiting the debtors with far less than they owed, he placed them unequivocally in his power. Since they were now involved in his own duplicity, he could, if the occasion demanded, exercise a little judicious blackmail. Here, without a doubt, was an unprincipled scoundrel! Yet Jesus commends him, saying, "For the children of this world are in their generation wiser than the children of light."

The early Church found this parable puzzling. Luke attached to it no less than three different interpretations. The first, "Make to yourselves friends of the mammon of unrighteousness" (verse 9), seems to imply that material possessions should be invested in making friendships which are more durable than perishable riches. The next, "He that is faithful in that which is least, is faithful also in much: and he that is unjust in the least is unjust also in much. If therefore ye have not been faithful in the unrighteous mammon, who will commit to your trust the true riches? And if ye have not been faithful in that which is another man's, who shall give you that which is your own?" (verses 10, 11 and 12), seems to teach that the way a man handles a small task is the best proof we have as to whether he is fit for larger responsibilities. Finally, "No servant can serve two masters: for either he will hate the one, and love the other; or else he will hold to the one, and despise the other. Ye cannot serve God and mammon" (verse 13), points to yet another moral—the danger of divided loyalty—the schizophrenic business of worshipping God and mammon.

According to certain New Testament scholars, the parable in its original form ends at verse 8. What Jesus is commending is not sharp practice—that surely is so obvious that we need not stress it—but alertness and astuteness and resolute action. He draws our attention to the incredible obtuseness and complacency of the devout, and their proneness where difficult issues are concerned to surrender the initiative to the irreligious. This then is the meaning of the words, "For the children of this world are in their generation wiser than the children of light."

This parable presses home the need for an intelligent appraisal of the situation. We are under no illusion whatsoever about the factor himself. Judged by any standard, his behaviour is inexcusable. He had been given a position of trust and he had betrayed it. This is so, but his initiative in the face of impending disaster wins our grudging admiration. Not only did he understand the psychology of those he had to deal with, but he managed by a combination of shrewd bargaining and prompt resoluteness to extricate himself from a crisis of the first magnitude.

Jesus, here, is hitting out at the Pharisees and the religious leaders of His day. Compared to the Romans and the Greeks, they were the children of light. Custodians of a great religious heritage, they had in their possession God's revelation of Himself through the law and the prophets. An *élite* corps, they were in a position to use this knowledge for the enlightenment of their own nation and the emancipation of mankind. But what did they do? They buried the truth under mountains of prohibitive regulations, they shut themselves in within a cramped little world of their own making, and they let the great dynamic movements of history by-pass them.

This is precisely our dilemma today. Custodians of the truth that became incarnate in Jesus Christ, we have allowed ourselves to be shunted off the main thoroughfare of life. Imprisoned within our own little religious world, we are impotent and frightened spectators of stupendous forces that are making history, over which we seem to exercise no control whatsoever.

We are told today that we live in "a post-Christian era"—a phrase which Dietrich Bonhoeffer passed into theological currency. What he meant is that we are witnessing the break-up of the integration of man's cultural life, which took a thousand years to build and another thousand to undo. Whether we agree with this claim or not does not make any material difference. While we are debating the point, our culture is being shaped by images and habits of thought which are no longer recognisably Christian.

Within the organised Church we give no impression that we have grasped this disturbing fact. We live in a different world where mothers' meetings, badminton clubs in church halls, and all the paraphernalia of congregational life, invested with ultimate sanctity, are not even remotely related to what is happening outside. We hate to be compared with the Pharisees of the New Testament, but at least we have this in common with them—our preoccupation with the wrong things, and blindness to the terrifying issues threatening our existence and clamouring for a profound religious answer.

This then is a precondition of our salvation—an intelligent appraisal of the situation—a clear-eyed recognition that for many influential leaders of thought, the traditional God is dead. The majority, who would hesitate to go as far, treat Him as a social adjunct or a cultural accessory, which means that for them, however much they deny it, He is dead also. The secularisation of modern culture and the Church's inability to check it, far less set the process in reverse—that is the crisis before which the children of light stand stricken and dumb and helpless.

Again, this parable presses home the need for a radical approach to the problem. The unjust steward, realising the seriousness of his predicament, spurned all half-way measures, and decided on a radical solution. The so-called debtors were wholesale merchants who had given promissory notes for goods received. To one of them who had received one hundred measures of oil he said, "I'll tell you what I'll do, I'll reduce your debt by half—call it fifty." To another he said, "You owe me a hundred measures of wheat—well here is a new agreement, make it eighty." The whole thing was highly unethical, but it swept the *status quo* aside, and radically transformed his relationship with his business associates.

Even the most complacent in our midst must admit that the Church is faced with a desperate situation, and in our efforts to meet it, two courses of action lie open to us. We can, on the one hand, carefully balance the pros and cons against one another and, conscious of the complexity of the situation, proceed with conspicuous caution. Or, on the other hand, we can emulate the unjust steward of the gospel, and come to grips with the problem with a bold and thorough-going radicalism.

Not even its bitterest enemies can accuse the Church of passive inertness today. Never before have we been more furiously active. Never before have we tried so many experiments or launched such well-organised campaigns. Never before have we used the organ of publicity—press, radio and television—so unashamedly, but the results are not at all commensurate with the vast sums of money, and the prodigous energy expended. Only a simpleton could claim that we have in any radical sense changed people's values, or altered the climate of opinion.

We desperately need a religious revival, but ask the average minister and the average church member what sort of revival he is looking for, and his answer at once reveals why conventional Christianity is so crassly ineffective in the twentieth century. He wants to see pews packed, Sunday honoured and observed, and the Church regaining its diminished social prestige. It never seems to occur to him that what he nostalgically longs for was an established fact in the heyday of Victorian religiosity, yet the Church neither anticipated the coming crisis, nor came to grips with the basic problems of that time.

Medical science is beginning to treat man in the totality of his being. The day when the body with its various aches and pains was all the doctor was concerned with, has happily disappeared. The psychosomatic emphasis—the recognition that man is a unity and that therefore there can be no artificial divorce between the spiritual and physical sides of his nature— is now, more or less, an article of medical orthodoxy. The Christian emphasis must be no less total. To spiritualise man in the old traditional sense is to devitalise him and it inevitably leads to an emasculation of Christianity. The only revival we can sincerely pray for is one which converts the individual and at the same time Christianises the social structures which help to shape and determine his behaviour. This means that in the most radical sense imaginable the Christian spirit must inform and inspire our politics, our culture and our education, indeed the whole range of our human relationships.

In conclusion, this parable of the unjust steward presses home the need for a prophetic anticipation of the future. The unjust steward did not wait till calamity, swift and irreversible, had caught up with him. He anticipated the crisis which his own dishonest actions had triggered off, and, by exercising foresight, he averted the judgment which was about to fall on him.

We are still apt to entertain the weirdest notions as to what prophecy means. We are prone to regard the prophets of the Bible as rather odd people endowed with psychic gifts of a peculiar nature—second-sight, pre-cognition, extra-sensory perception, or whatever we prefer to call it. To be sure, men like Ezekiel may have been genuinely psychic, but what distinguishes the great prophets like Isaiah and Jeremiah is not that, but their ability to discern the signs of the time, their uncanny sense of anticipation, enabling them to see the shape of things to come and to declare with authority, "Thus saith the Lord".

The Biblical faith essentially is a prophetic faith. Jesus, the greatest of all the prophets, while He respected all that was good in tradition, never allowed it to stand in the way. It was because He was a bold and intrepid pathfinder blazing a trail through the thick undergrowth of an obstructive traditionalism that the Establishment did away with Him. The Reformation was a recovery of this prophetic faith, and once Protestantism loses it, it is no better than a reactionary sect, noisily protesting in order to justify its own dubious existence.

The truth is that the secular conscience at its sharpest is away out ahead of the Church today. On practically every crucial issue that calls for an intelligent appraisal, a radical approach, a prophetic awareness, the best of the secularists beat us to it. They are out in front formulating solutions, while we are feebly reacting to situations in the rear, and still we are surprised and pained that the world refuses to take us very seriously.

Examples of the Church's non-prophetic role in the twentieth century are so numerous that the difficulty is one of selection. I confine myself to two. Consider Church unity, which we must regard no longer as a luxury, but as an indispensable necessity. While it is true that since the war our conscience has been awakened on this issue, it is equally true we are dragging our feet and haggling over trivialities. We talk as if events like Amsterdam, Evanston and New Delhi were veritable miracles. What a wonderful thing it is, we effuse, to see Christians from different nations and divergent traditions meeting together in the spirit of brotherliness; and we expect the world to clap its hands, and give us a congratulatory cheer. The proper retort is surely, "What do ye more than others?" Scientists and economists have been doing the same for decades without indulging in unseemly self-congratulation. I suspect that Europe will have arrived at economic unity, and Russian and American scientists will be exploring outer space together before the Churches will have reconciled their differences.

Or consider the emancipation of women. It is now taken for granted almost everywhere except in the Church. Science had accepted it, so have politics and medicine, journalism and business. But the Church of Rome, the Church of England and the Church of Scotland still remain adamant. In time they too will be forced to come to terms, but a cynical world will not credit them with any sense of prophetic anticipation:

> There is a tide in the affairs of men,
> Which, taken at the flood, leads on to fortune;
> Omitted, all the voyage of their life
> Is bound in shallows and in miseries.

In our low moods when we are tempted to believe that the Church is the most moribund of all institutions, we must remember that the Christ who died and rose again is our living contemporary. He expounded His parables in Galilee some two thousand years ago, but no matter how far we progress in personal morality and social idealism, we can never advance beyond Him who was the Pioneer of Life. He pleads with us not to let our fondness of the past set limits to our understanding of the future. He enjoins us as the children of light to stand expectant and alert, prophetically anticipating the will of God as it unfolds itself in history.

E

2

THE PARABLE OF
THE TARES

ST. MATTHEW 13, 14–20

THE tare is a name for a weed called darnel which grows in Palestine to this day. In its early stages it was impossible to distinguish it from wheat. Once it had headed out, the difference was obvious, but by that time the roots of the two were so inextricably entangled that any attempt to remove the one resulted in tearing up the other by the roots. As a rule the separation of the wheat from the darnel weed was left till after the threshing.

The parable indicates that the poisonous weed called darnel was planted, not accidentally, but with malicious intent. This is not a dramatic prop used to drive home one main truth. It is based on actual fact. In the ancient world, where men were at least as vindictive as they are now, one of the commonest ways of venting spite was to sow bad seed in another man's ground. In ancient Palestine, where only a miserable existence could be eked out of the soil, such an act could be fearfully damaging.

"An enemy hath done this." The words remind us of the grim reality of evil in the world. Here we are made to face up to the brute fact that there is in history a malevolent force which deliberately seeks to sabotage the purpose of God. Whatever name we give it—devil, Satan, or collective iniquity, there is no doubt that such a power does exist. It is impossible to explain away the last two wars and the present threat of total annihilation in terms of maladjustment alone. It looks as if there were a saboteur at work behind the lines, sowing the seeds of discord, planting the poison of suspicion and thwarting our holiest efforts to establish the order of our dreams upon the earth. The philosopher, Berdyaev, is surely right when he claims that there is a demonic element in modern history. When we contemplate our strained international relationships and consider how human ingenuity and national wealth are squandered on developing weapons of destruction, we can only say "an enemy hath done this". This parable speaks powerfully to our contemporary situation.

For one thing, it speaks to the dilemma of politics. Whatever our political bias we are all deeply concerned with the clash between East and West, between communism on the one hand and democracy on the other. This is no academic problem or a subject for idle speculation. It is a struggle between two mighty opposites, literally a matter of life and death. Our own country is spending a fabulous sum of money on weapons which are obsolete before they can be mass produced. If fear of Russia were to subside, taxation could be slashed, the cost of living would assume more sensible proportions and we could at last afford to set in motion a revolutionary system of education, able to harness the total intellectual vitality of Britain.

What is the sane attitude to the problem of communism, or if we prefer to put it another way, what is the Christian approach? Are we to regard it as a deadly weed planted in the soil of western civilisation by the enemies of God? Are its leaders determined to do away with the Church and every democratic institution which seems to nourish freedom and protect the sanctity of the individual?

Now, there are those among us who believe that Russian communism is unqualifiedly and absolutely evil. It is of the Devil, they say, and compromise with it is impossible. They are thick on the ground in this country, and considerably more so in America. To them, a policy of co-existence is not merely distasteful, it is a downright denial of democracy and a betrayal of the Christian religion. Why compromise with evil and give it a chance to consolidate itself? Why enter into diplomatic relations with the Devil, they ask? Better take the risk, go to war now and tear this satanic growth up by the roots.

That, at least, is one possible attitude to the problem, but such a programme, if we examine it, is bedevilled by two weaknesses. On the one hand, it is guilty of a black and white mentality. It assumes that communism is on the side of the Devil and that democracy is on the side of the angels. I cannot see how any intelligent Christian can subscribe to such a patently false belief. The democracy I am familiar with is tainted and partially corrupt, and I suspect that communism, however inhuman and compounded with evil, does contain some good. The truth is that the roots of good and evil in the complex of human relationships we call society are so hopelessly intertwined that in practice it is not possible to separate them. The parable seems to advocate a policy of co-existence, and where communism is concerned this would seem to be the sane and Christian attitude.

On the other hand, suppose we were to declare war on communism and try to eradicate it from our world. That would involve the use of atomic weapons, resulting in something approaching total annihilation. How supremely up-to-date and topical the parable of the tares is! In trying to destroy communism, an atomic war would only succeed in tearing up civilisation and organised Christianity by the roots. The logic of the situation is irrefutable. We must allow the two diverging political systems to co-exist together in the world and leave the ultimate judgment to God.

For another thing, this parable speaks to the dilemma of religion. In the first instance this parable was expounded as an answer to certain criticisms levelled at Christ's tolerance. His own disciples, brought up as orthodox Jews, accepted the traditional belief that the Messiah, when He came, would establish the pure community of God's elect. Therefore they found it difficult to understand why Jesus welcomed all sorts and conditions of men. Some of His followers were socially far from reputable, and morally they left a great deal to be desired. John the Baptist was so strict and exclusive in his emphasis—why was Jesus so incredibly tolerant?

If the disciples were puzzled, the Pharisees were

shocked. They regarded themselves as the holy community, the elect of God, and they looked upon the masses as the children of darkness. They were outraged by Christ's behaviour. How did He expect them to listen to Him when He sat down with publicans and sinners, and included among His friends men like Matthew and Zaccheus, the tax collectors, and even a notorious ex-prostitute like Mary Magdalene. Even more galling was the fact that Jesus declared war on their "holy community" belief, and preferred the company of social and moral outcasts.

That has been the dilemma of religion all along. All schisms within the Church, all sectarian revolts and splintered groups, are due to this separatist mentality. Its aim is to exclude from the Church all those who deviate from the rigid requirements set down. Much better, they argue, to have a dedicated minority, an *élite* corps, a faithful nucleus, than to throw the doors of the Church open to all and sundry. Some of the sects are logical enough to try and put this policy into practice. They pride themselves on their caste and exclusiveness and sneer at the established Church as the refuge of all the spiritual dregs of society.

If we examined this policy of exclusiveness from the standpoint of the New Testament, and especially in the light of this parable, we find it is untenable for various reasons. For one thing, its advocates forget that the Church can never be pure because the roots of good and evil in society are so desperately mixed up. The purest of sects are tainted by evil. The more they seek to separate themselves from the world, the more ineffective and impotent they become in society.

But the chief count against exclusiveness in religion is that it is a stupifying and self-defeating policy. When men set themselves up as judges, they arrogate to themselves an attribute which belongs only to God. The Pharisee is the greatest of all sinners precisely because he does not regard himself as a sinner, and considers himself morally superior to others. It would 'be tempting sometimes to get rid of all the awkward people in the Church, the whiners, the slackers, the hangers-on, but we would end with having a set of obnoxious, pious prigs, an abomination in the sight of God. The truth is that Christians who seek to drive the bad people out of the Church succeed only in being worse than the people they seek to eject. The message of this parable is profound and salutary—good and evil will exist, side by side within the Church to the end of time. Separation would mean the tearing up of Christianity by the roots.

Finally, this parable speaks to the dilemma of personality. In human nature there is a radical twist—a principle of contradiction, a fundamental bias towards evil. Even the most passionate idealists are aware of this hiatus between aspiration and achievement. No one has expressed the problem more pungently than Paul—"The good that I would I do not, and the evil that I would not, that I do."

Towards this basic split in personality various attitudes are possible. There is the attitude of moral anarchy which advocates indiscipline and takes pride in obeying the dictates of every aggressive drive and every impulse of passion. No society has ever been able to tolerate such people for long. Community demands a coherent structure, and for the purpose of self-preservation it insists on a certain measure of moral discipline.

At the other end of the moral spectrum, we find the perfectionists who have an exaggerated, one might say a pathological, sense of guilt. Weakness in any shape or form is anathema to them, and to eradicate it from their nature they are prepared to go to any extreme. According to a well-known psychologist, most of his patients throughout his professional career have been moral perfectionists and they are by far the most difficult to cure. They project for themselves an ideal of perfection and are prepared to move heaven and earth to attain it. This explains the high incidence of nervous breakdown among them.

The truth is that perfectionism is the deadliest of all forms of egotism. It is the refusal to accept one's self, a shutting of the eyes to the tensions, contradictions, temptations, and thorns in the flesh that must buffet and inevitably frustrate us. It is a secret wish to be like God, and this is the apex of human pride. However disappointing we may find it, the truth is that personality can never be completely free of sin this side of time. The perfectionist, in trying to tear up the tares of his conflicts and complexes, succeeds only in tearing up the wheat of his sanity and stability.

The Christian answer is very different. Realistically it accepts sin as part and parcel of our make up—the tares rooted in human nature—but it does not accept it in a spirit of docile and passive acquiescence. The Christian resents this evil intrusion. He says—"An enemy hath done this," but while he knows he can never get rid of it this side of time, he sees to it that the wheat of salvation gets a chance to grow and proliferate in order to keep the tares of sin in check. The important thing to remember is that we cannot enter into right relationship with God by working our own passage. After all, a parent does not wait till his child is a little perfectionist before he loves him. (Some of us would have to wait a long time.) No, we love our children despite their faults, and if there is love possible on a human plane, how much more so on that of the Divine.

The important point to grasp is that the accent of this parable is on the positive, not on the negative. Despite the tares in the midst, the wheat will grow and a harvest will be reaped. So it is with the Kingdom of God. Nothing will ultimately impede its growth. And so it is with individual salvation. The tares, in the shape of sin, will ever be rooted in our nature, but nevertheless by the grace of God we can become new creatures in Christ "Who is able to keep you from falling and to present you faultless before the presence of His glory with exceeding joy, to the only wise God, our Saviour, be glory and majesty, dominion and power, both now and ever. *Amen.*

3

THE PARABLE OF
THE GOOD SAMARITAN

ST. LUKE 10, 30–37

THE mere telling of this story demonstrates among other things the moral courage of Jesus. His audience was truculently Jewish, therefore He must have known He would incur resentment and hostility. What modern parallel can we think of? It was as if at the height of the McCarthy Inquisition in America, a prominent citizen were to announce that in his opinion the American way of life was not so marvellous after all, and then went on to claim that Communists *vis-à-vis* the problems convulsing our world were more intelligent and more compassionate than Christians. Perhaps we can imagine then the reaction of those who first heard Jesus expound the parable of the Good Samaritan.

In the past this parable has been treated as a cryptic code message, the deciphering of which demanded a key for every single detail of the story. It was regarded as an allegory pure and simple, therefore there were no limits to the number of possible interpretations. Perhaps the most notorious example of this allegorical treatment is found in the preaching of Augustine. According to him, the man who was attacked was none other than Adam himself. Jerusalem is the Heavenly city from whose blessedness the sinful Adam fell. Jericho is the moon, signifying mortality, because it waxes and wanes and dies. The thieves are the Devil and his angels. The inn is the Church, and the innkeeper the apostle Paul. No one can question Augustine's genius, but his interpretation of this parable, while it is original, is not too conspicuously intelligent.

The allegorising habit dies hard: it has persisted from New Testament times and it is even prevalent today, when with so much biblical scholarship at our disposal we ought to know better. This emerges in a recent book on the Parables by Helmut Thielike—a man who combines profound scholarship with a preaching gift of the highest degree. In his sermon on the Good Samaritan he seems to me to attach too much significance to the various details of the story. Not only does he draw a distinction between the priest and the Levite, but he actually argues that the phrase "passed by on the other side" indicates that the priest was trying to placate a restive conscience, which is surely a piece of fanciful embroidery.

We can dispense with allegory when we remember that the wealth of detail—the robber-infested road, the two cities, Jerusalem and Jericho, the priest, the Levite, the inn and all the rest—are no more than dramatic machinery—so many stage props in the hands of Jesus, the Supreme Artist, to help Him project one central truth. They serve one purpose—to focus the searchlight on the Samaritan coming to the rescue of a fellow human in need. The inner nerve of the parable is exposed by a question which still stabs us to the quick and clamours for a clear and unequivocal answer. Who is my neighbour?

To grasp the real point of the question we must place it in its original setting. Traditional enemies, the Jews despised the Samaritans, because the latter were of mixed blood and in the eyes of the purists an inferior race. The relation between the two peoples, never good at the best of times, had deteriorated as a result of an incident which took place about A.D. 9, and with which Jesus was no doubt familiar. At Passover time the Samaritans had defiled the Temple Court by littering it with dead men's bones—an unforgivable sin in the eyes of orthodox Jews. By making a despised half-breed the hero of the piece, Jesus is declaring war on every form of entrenched prejudice. At the same time He is declaring that a Christian must regard every man in need as his neighbour and must act accordingly.

There is an inescapable sense in which modern science has thrust proximity upon us, but proximity divorced from community is a very dangerous business. The annihilation of distance has made the peoples of the world cheek-by-jowl neighbours, whether they like it or not. Physically this is so, but psychologically and spiritually they may live poles apart. The lawyer who first posed this famous question was no doubt being sarcastic at the expense of an untutored village carpenter. Jesus in his brilliant reply demonstrated, not only to him but to posterity, that this is a fundamental question which probes under the surface right to the heart of things.

Who is my neighbour? This question is thrust on us

by the problem of race today. When Jesus told this disconcerting story, racial discrimination was rampant. And so quite deliberately He makes the Samaritan the hero of the parable because the Jews regarded themselves as an élite people. The message He intends to convey is simply this—Christian love is blind to the composition of a man's blood or to the colour of his skin. It treats all men as brothers because it recognises that they have God as their Father.

If racialism was a burning issue in the first century, it is an explosive one in the twentieth, and there can be no solution if men are not prepared to approach the dilemma with a mixture of intelligence and charity. Only diehards who cannot discern the signs of the time believe that the demand for recognition on the part of the suppressed races can only be met with force. That is why the cast-iron South African formula approaches the ultimate in blindness and imbecility.

If I were to allegorise this parable, I would equate the suppressed races with the wounded man lying on the road. And I would be strongly tempted to equate the thugs and thieves who beat him up, with the so-called civilised nations who, in the past, sold them into slavery and wantonly exploited them to further their own economic interests. In the last century Britain fought a war against China in order to force her to buy the opium she did not want. Our pious Victorian fathers excused this odious brand of devilry on the ground that the Chinese were a primitive and inferior race. The solution Jesus advocates in this parable is the only practical one, and sooner or later we shall have to accept it. The different races must aim not merely at a precarious policy of co-existence, but also at a programme of mutual co-operation and Christian neighbourliness.

Who is my neighbour? Again this question is thrust upon us by the problem of nationalism. A narrow, exclusive, nationalistic loyalty is the sworn enemy of Christianity which from the very beginning proclaimed a universal Gospel. It has induced men to commit every crime in the calendar, and it has been responsible for some of the most brutal and most unjust wars in history. Politicians who in private life are pillars of moral rectitude, are prepared in the interests of their own country to stoop to every form of intrigue and duplicity. This is the fact which Reinhold Niebuhr so mercilessly expounds in his book, *Moral Man in Immoral Society*.

In the atomic age, nationalism is the sort of luxury we can no longer afford, so it is not surprising that responsible men in every country are seriously talking in terms of world government. Even those of us who cannot go all the way with Bertrand Russell in all his emphases, feel he is right in his blistering condemnation of nationalism. Avowed sceptic though he is, he is proclaiming something which is essentially Christian when he pleads for a political system which transcends our squalid acquisitiveness and our outmoded conceptions of sovereignty. That is why I agree so strongly with Britain's bid to join the Common Market.

Nationalism in its most gruesome guise is seen in the unholy scramble to join the nuclear club. This costly ambition on the part of the less powerful nations is motivated not so much by fear as by the desire for prestige. The possession of the hydrogen bomb has become the status symbol *par excellence*. And where Russia and America are concerned, I fancy that their prodigious efforts to project humans into orbit round the earth were not entirely dictated by scientific considerations, but were compounded of national pride and jingoistic glory. Nationalism is a dangerous idol, a devouring Moloch with an insatiable appetite for human sacrifice. Ah, Christ how far-seeing you were! In an age when we all tremble under the threat of nuclear disaster it is easy for us to recoil from nationalism, but two thousand years ago you attacked this evil fetish in the parable of the Good Samaritan and you exposed it for the dirty, devilish, murderous thing it undeniably is.

Who is my neighbour? This question, sharply focussed for us by racialism and nationalism, is finally thrust upon us by the problem of class. Whoever said that the class war is dead is simply deluding himself. It is not. The truth is that people spend more of their ingenuity and nervous energy in scrambling up the ladder of class than on anything else. Read Vance Packard's book, *The Hidden Persuaders*, and it becomes clear that in America the deliberate exploiting of class consciousness is one of the most rewarding discoveries made by the advertising industry. Products from cars to cigarette lighters sell well if the advertisers manage to convey as delicately as possible that they possess snob value. Indeed Packard goes further and asserts that in modern America the achievement drive and the compulsive urge to acquire social standing, are in a large measure responsible for the high incidence of neurosis and nervous breakdown.

In Britain the urge to move up the social ladder may not be so strong, but the reason for this is not that we are more virtuous than the Americans, but that we are less enterprising. More moulded by tradition, we tend to accept rigid social stratifications as part of the national landscape. The problem of class is not confined to any one country—it is universal because it is rooted in pride which is the parent sin.

Class consciousness, however cunningly camouflaged it may be, is the avowed enemy of a real Christian community. We need not look for any facile solution, because the psychology of snobbery is very puzzling and complex. I have never met anyone so far who does not deplore a snob. In our society the snob is an object of ridicule and supercilious scorn, yet those who loudly condemn would fight ferociously to preserve the social structures which make snobbishness and class awareness possible. Jesus, in this parable, was hitting where it hurt most, when in terms of sensitiveness and humanity he exalted a Samaritan half-breed above the proud members of an *élite* class.

This parable is not exclusively addressed to the priestly caste of the first century; it speaks to all of us and it asks us to examine our own deeply-entrenched, long-established sanctified prejudices. As Christians, we too have passed by on the other side of practically every agonising issue in the twentieth century, and how can we expect to eradicate the ingrained attitudes of centuries from our world till first we conquer them in ourselves?

Jesus is asking us to demonstrate Christian compassion in a practical manner. The Samaritan was not just touched with pity, he bound up the wounds of the stricken man and provided for his most pressing needs. The emotion of pity is only genuine when it is prepared to translate itself into specific action. And today that means immersing ourselves in politics, social concern, and various humanitarian projects.

However desperate the situation, charity infused with imagination and informed with intelligence can find a way out. In citing the example of Vinoba, the Indian saint on whose shoulders the prophetic mantle of Gandhi fell, I am being true to the spirit of the parable. Realising that India's No. 1 enemy was poverty, he has dedicated his life to the task of persuading the rich to give up their lands to the poor, and in this he has been astonishingly successful. With no staff, no organisation and no publicity, he goes on foot from village to village, interviewing princes and urging them to help the needy. Since 1931 he has walked nearly 30,000 miles. Already he has got 8,000,000 acres, representing only a modest percentage of his ultimate target of 50,000,000. The situation calling out in our country is very different, but it is no less challenging. With the example of Grenfell of Labrador, Kagawa of Japan, Schweitzer in Africa, Vinoba in India, who in their own different ways re-enacted the parable of the Good Samaritan, it is difficult to shut our ears to the incisiveness of our Lord's command, "Go and do thou likewise".

4

THE PARABLE OF
THE TALENTS

OF all the parables, this is one of the best known, but also one of the most misunderstood. Its interpretation seems so straightforward and so obvious that it has been used as a springboard for all sorts of oversimplified philosophies and conventional prejudices.

It has been used to justify financial investment, speculation on the Stock Exchange and every form of gambling. This, of course, is absurd. Jesus expounded the parable not as a moral investor's guide, but to draw our attention to a truth which belongs to the very meaning of life and to the inner nature of human personality.

It has been used to deny the classical Christian doctrine of the equality of all men in the sight of God and, at a superficial glance, this would appear to be so. In the parable Jesus seems to acknowledge varying degrees of ability. One man is superbly equipped with five talents, and prospers accordingly. A second man, while not brilliant, is adequately endowed and does full justice to his opportunities. But the third begins life with a crippling handicap and consequently falls out in the gruelling competitive race. What, may we ask, can anyone do with one paltry, miserable talent?

This, I am sure, is a gross travesty of the parable. The doctrine of the equality of all men in the sight of God never did imply equality of ability. Whatever we may say, history pooh-poohs any such theory by throwing up its Pauls, its Shakespeares, its Beethovens, who tower above their fellows in natural endowment. This fact cannot be denied, but it does not in any real sense contradict the other fact that potentially all men despite varying talents, are equally important to God. Therefore, they must be given equal opportunities to develop and express themselves.

It is significant that in this parable the spotlight falls not on the men with the five and the two talents, but on the man with the one. The others are no more than artistic props, dramatic machinery used by the Master Artist Himself to throw the man of one talent into bolder prominence. So the thing to note is that the one talent man is neither a criminal nor a knave, but a misguided, muddle-headed fool, whose thinking is twisted because his vision of reality is out of focus. This parable drives home to us certain truths it is folly to ignore.

The first is the importance of a right conception of God. Why did the man of one talent go and bury it in the ground instead of investing it profitably like the other two? He behaved this way, the parable makes clear, because he misunderstood his employer and carried about with him a false impression of his character. "I know thee that thou art an hard man, reaping where thou hast not sown and gathering where

thou hast not strawed, and I was afraid and went and
hid thy talent in the earth."

The Pharisees were the living embodiment of this
truth. Far from being atheists, they believed in God
with a fierce and passionate intensity. Yet they were the
very men who perpetrated the most shocking crime in
history. They hounded Christ to the Cross, not because
they were by nature cruel and sadistic, but because
they were wrong about the character of God. They
regarded Him not as a forgiving father, but as a hard
master imposing on human shoulders burdens too heavy
to be borne. Consequently, their relationship to Him
was characterised by fear, furtiveness and craven dis-
trust.

We could indeed argue, with a considerable degree of
cogency, that a mistaken view of the nature of ultimate
reality is responsible for all the major crimes in history
—the caste system in India, the social inequalities of
Islam, the savagery of the Nazis, the materialism of
the communists, and the petty-minded sectarianism
so rampant in conventional Christianity. In the long
run, it is not possible to divorce creed from conduct.
What we believe in our hearts will sooner or later
express itself in our behaviour.

Arnold Toynbee, the historian, pleads for a sensible
synthesis of all that is best in the various religions.
Instead of puzzling our brains with the baffling paradox
of the Incarnation, he would have us content ourselves
with a belief in a cosmic intelligence giving meaning to
the enigma of our human existence.

But the problem is by no means as simple as this.

for even more important than the question of the existence of God is that of His character. This was precisely the experience of C. S. Lewis who, from being
an avowed agnostic, came to believe in God. But no
sooner had he found an answer to one question than
he found himself wrestling with another. What is the
nature of the God I have come to acknowledge? Where,
if anywhere, have all the hints and clues and glimpses
of man's spiritual striving found fulfilment? And,
immediately, for Lewis the absolute centrality of Christ
took on a new meaning.

The basic claim of the Christian faith is that God,
in His character, is like Jesus. "If God," cried Stanley
Jones, "is like Jesus, He is good enough for me. I want
none other." Christians believe that the persons who
taught and healed in Galilee, who agonised in prayer
in Gethsemane, who died forgiving His enemies on the
Cross, is the perfect mirror of the nature of ultimate
Reality. Christ alone gives us a true picture of
God.

The second truth this parable drives home is the
importance of intelligent enterprise. Without intelligent enterprise, no civilisation, no science, no progress
is possible. Without the willingness to take risks, the
world would still be what A. N. Whitehead describes as, "an uninterpreted swamp, pestilential with
magic and mystery". Without this ineradicable instinct
to reach out beyond the familiar, there would have
been no discovery of America, no jets in the skies, no
venturing into outer space. Animals are perfectly
adjusted to their environment. They chew their cud

contentedly undisturbed by unattainable dreams. Man, on the other hand, is a restless, tormented creature in whom burns an instinct for the unknown.

Jesus, when He expounded this parable, was specifically addressing Himself to the Pharisees. They had drained religion of the spirit of enterprise in any shape or form and had fenced it about with all sorts of inhibitions. Their accent was entirely on the past, and a prophetic anticipation of things to come was not only strongly frowned on but ruthlessly suppressed. They represent the third man in the parable, for they took the God-given talent of faith and, instead of using it intelligently, they buried it in the earth of a formal and moribund ecclesiasticism.

In this sense most Christians today are Pharisees not because they are consciously insincere and hypocritical, but because they are not enterprising and are prepared to risk little or nothing in the name of Christ. Like the New Testament Pharisees, they are quite content with perpetuating the traditional patterns of Church life and shutting their eyes to the pressing demands of the present and the agonising challenges of the future. This attitude, all too prevalent amongst elders, members and ministers, is to be condemned on three counts. It is un-Christian, it doesn't work, and in the end it leads to disaster.

This parable exposes the greatest weakness of the Church of Scotland—its inability to translate secular ability into spiritual coinage. Ours is a layman's Church—theoretically at least—and logically you might argue that the multitude of professors and doctors,

teachers, lawyers, bankers, accountants, writers and
business executives, would see to it that the Church
is the most progressive institution in the land. But this
kind of thinking is based on the fallacy that the Church
member transfers his ability from his business or
profession over to the Church, that he is as intelligent
in the spiritual as he is in the secular sense. This is a
myth which does not bear scrutiny.

Knowing voices within the Church of England tell
us that it is now a fashionable pose for many to be
ultra-conservative within the Church in the measure
in which they are dynamic and progressive outside it.
Their minds are open to change everywhere else, but
where faith is concerned, things must remain the same
yesterday, today and for ever.

This, surely, is the inner nerve and meaning of
Christian Stewardship. It is not wheedling more money
out of unwilling pockets. It is not spending more of our
time perpetuating patterns of Church life that God is
pleading with us to discard. It is not multiplying
useless and meaningless organisations and giving our
blessing to the cult of activism. No. On the contrary,
Stewardship really means the enterprising use of our
talents—the intelligent grappling with questions which
demand immediate answers. It means the ruthless
examination of our traditional attitudes and the opening
of our minds to new ideas.

There is one final truth which this parable drives
home and it is this: that what we do not use, we lose.
The man with the one talent went and hid it in the
ground, thinking it would be safe there. Ironically

enough, he was the only one of the three that in the end lost it. He put his trust in the wrong kind of security. He played safe and lost and was openly discredited. This is more than a picturesque metaphor: it is an incontestable fact. It illustrates an iron, inexorable law that runs right through the whole of our human existence. It decrees that what we don't use, we lose.

This is true physically, psychologically, spiritually. During the war I became friends with an officer who was a magnificent specimen of physical fitness. He excelled at endurance tests, and sixty miles a day with full kit he could take in his stride. Recently I went climbing with him and, to my surprise, I found that he had gone to seed. The most modest peaks utterly exhausted him. During ten years of a sedentary occupation, his lungs and muscles had gone flabby. What we don't use, we lose.

In Charles Darwin's autobiography we come across a pathetic confession. As a young man he derived great pleasure from poetry and music. But his intense preoccupation with science soon crowded out these interests. In his old age he eagerly turned to them again, looking for a measure of spiritual comfort, but, to his sorrow, found that he had lost his aptitude. What we do not use, we lose.

All men have been endowed with a talent for religion. Our capacity for communion with God belongs to the very meaning of our humanity. But most of us, like the man in the parable, foolishly imagine we can bury it in the earth of a casual indifference and dig it up whenever we want it. What we fail to see is that our awareness of God may become increasingly dim, our vision of the unseen progressively blurred, and our capacity for things spiritual more limited as time passes. What we don't use, we lose.

The point of this parable of the talents is not the rather wearisome truism that a man ought to use his gifts to the full. It strikes a much more urgent note. It tells us that life is never static, that, in order to cope with it, we must be alert and courageously progressive. The accent from first to last is on the need to decide and act intelligently. In this story of the buried talents we are confronted with the challenge of an intelligent use of our possessions and abilities. The question the parable asks is one which no Christian can sidestep. Have you invested your God-given endowments in an enterprising and courageous commitment?

5

THE PARABLE OF
THE LEAVEN

ST. LUKE 13, 20, 21

"And again he said, Whereunto shall I liken the
Kingdom of God? It is like leaven which a woman
took and hid in three measures of meal, till the
whole was leavened."

JESUS had often watched a woman baking bread. The
process was very simple. She took a large quantity of
meal and into the centre of the mass she inserted a small
portion of yeast. In time, the heavy lump of dough
changed its appearance, becoming light, porous and
spongy. In this simple domestic practice, Jesus saw a
vivid picture of the way the Kingdom of God grows
and spreads in history. "It is," He said, "like leaven
which a woman took and hid in three measures of meal,
till the whole was leavened."

The parable reminds us of the power of a dedicated,
militant minority. Whatever the problem under con-
sideration, cancer, colonisation, or the drinking habits
of people, there is an insistent demand for facts and
figures. We want to know how high the incidence is,
how many thousands of millions think in a certain
fashion; what evidence we possess for the persistence of
certain trends, hence the popularity of the Gallup poll

as a way of measuring public opinion. Statistics have ceased to be an amiable fad and have become an indispensable branch of modern science.

We see this when we begin to examine the problem of evangelism. All recent studies in this country and elsewhere have leaned heavily on statistics. In their book, *English Life and Leisure*, Messrs. Rowntree and Lavers, on the basis of a census they took in York in 1948, estimate that less than 10 per cent of the population of England attend church with any degree of regularity. And speaking for the Church of Scotland John Highet in his book, *The Scottish Churches*, assesses the average attendance on a Sunday as 12·7 of the total adult population; while C. E. M. Joad in his last book, *The Recovery of Belief*, writes, "It is not merely that only one in ten of the population of contemporary Britain have any continuing connection with the Church, more to the point is the fact that the 10 per cent includes a very high proportion of elderly and comparatively uneducated women."

Now while we must not be complacent about these figures, at the same time we must not be unduly depressed by them, for the New Testament emphasis is never on bigness but on vitality; never on quantity but on quality; never on dough but on leaven. Statistics and Gallup polls have their place in any society, but to invest them with a cast-iron infallibility leads in the end not only to a misreading of history, but also to the grossest forms of self-deception. The great liberating movements of the past were launched not by crushing majorities but by compact, militant minorities, the fermenting leaven at the heart of the collective lump.

This is true politically. How utterly insignificant Gandhi looked when first he played with the idea of liberating India. No sooner had he announced it than his enemies mounted a campaign of ridicule. He was caricatured as a toothless, spindly-legged, oriental mystic, wandering from place to place in a loincloth, an eccentric and an ascetic who indulged in protracted facts, an utterly unrealistic Utopian dreamer. More than once they threw him into prison, but try as they would, they could not crush the idea he stood for. Like leaven, it worked silently and potently, moulding and kneading the dough of Indian public opinion into shape, till at last it became irresistible, and Britain, with commendable wisdom, gave way.

It is also true intellectually. All the big momentous discoveries of history were, to begin with, opposed by the majority of people. Today, when everybody accepts the law of gravity without question, it is difficult to believe that the man who first propounded it, Isaac Newton, was cruelly lampooned and even persecuted. The critics accused him of a "deranged poetic fancy", and so disheartened was Newton by the storm of abuse, that in a despondent mood he once wrote, "I see a man must resolve to put out nothing new, or become a slave to defend it." But the idea he brought to light acted like leaven working its way through the dough of a tenaciously-held tradition, till within one century every educated person in the world had accepted it.

And it is certainly true spiritually. The Christian

Church with her millions of members spread across the earth surely demonstrates the truth of this parable. Around Jesus in Galilee a few enthusiasts gathered and what an unkempt, bedraggled, unimpressive lot they looked! What chance had this insignificant band against Caesar's mail-clad legions thundering their way across the earth, and how futile their ambitions seemed in face of the weighty councils of a mighty empire! Surely the Christian Church, her survival, and her continuing triumphant existence, is the supreme miracle; and it all stemmed from the leaven Jesus planted in the massive dough of history in the shape of a few dedicated disciples.

This would seem to indicate that our strategy of evangelism is far from sound. We are obsessed with size and statistics, and we have not accepted the truth which the prophet Isaiah proclaimed, that God acts best not through sprawling hosts but through a select remnant in whom the truth is clearly focussed and powerfully concentrated. Never was the Church more effective than when she was a dynamic nucleus spreading the leaven of her influence through the whole of society. If the New Testament and Church history are any guide, we must learn to put our faith not on the quantitatively huge but on the qualitatively small.

Again, the parable reminds us of the essential nature of Christian revolution. According to C. H. Dodd, we are wrong to suppose that here Jesus is teaching that religion is a quiet, steady, unobtrusive influence in society. He is in fact saying the very opposite. Dodd writes, "We should observe that the working of leaven in the dough is not a slow, imperceptible process. At first it is true that the leaven is hidden and that nothing appears to happen, but soon the whole mass swells and bubbles as fermentation rapidly advances. Just as the leaven turns the dough into a seething mass, so Christianity rightly understood is a disturbing thing."

Christ Himself is the living embodiment of this truth. There was a time when Protestant theologians painted a picture of Him as the benign Teacher come, not with the sword of challenge, but with the sweet balm of comfort, giving us in the Sermon on the Mount, the distilled wisdom of the ages. This portrait was popular till Albert Schweitzer wrote his *Quest for the Historical Jesus* and irreverently tore it to tatters. Jesus, argued Schweitzer, was not primarily a dispassionate philosopher, or a detached teacher, nor yet a mild reformer dedicated to the cult of benevolent humanitarianism. He was a flaming revolutionary who came not to prune a branch here and there, but to put the axe of radical change to the root of the existing order. It was because Jesus, in no uncertain manner, questioned the basic presuppositions on which the society of His time rested that He incurred the bitter hostility of all the forces of establishment. William Temple is more or less saying the same thing when he writes with some asperity, "Why any man should have troubled to crucify the Christ of liberal Protestantism has always been a mystery."

The Church is the cell Jesus left behind Him in the world to ferment and permeate the whole of history with the leaven of her influence. Once the Church ceases to disturb, she ceases to count, no matter how imposing her power or impressive her prestige. This is what happened in Russia within living memory: the Greek Orthodox Church allied herself with the existing *status quo*. It relinquished its prophetic mission and became the religious right arm of a corrupt political system. Therefore, when the Czarist regime collapsed in a welter of blood and terror, the national Church went down with it.

It is a truism to say that we live in an age of revolution, but most Christians behave as if this were not so. They have not grasped that we are in the throes of a second industrial revolution which is advancing with unexampled speed, leaving in its wake a host of problems —conduct, population, food, education—all clamouring for a practical solution. And unless our Gospel is related to these issues, it has nothing of importance to say to the malaise of modern man. It is estimated that a million new scientific facts are discovered every year, and thanks to technology these are soon in use, transforming our everyday world and conditioning our entire system of values. Mr. Khrushchev claims that this marriage between science and technology is the progenitor of all future progress, that it is the only god which can at one and the same time command our intellectual respect and our emotional allegiance.

What does the Christian say to such a creed, sponsored as it is by so many intelligent humanists inside and outside the communist world? First of all he must accept technology, not as an enemy of God, but as a

new development relevant to the Christian doctrine
of creation, which in the hands of good men can be used
as a tool for the shaping of the Kingdom of Heaven on
earth. The thing to grasp is that technology and the
kind of world it brings us into, has come to stay, and a
wistful hankering after the primitive simplicities of a
bygone age is the kind of nonsense which is neither
relevant nor tolerable.

On the other hand, Christians hold that a spiritual
revolution must go hand in hand with a secular revolution. Unless this is so, the end will be the macabre way
of life depicted by Aldous Huxley in his *Brave New
World*, and George Orwell in his *1984*. It is possible to
revolutionise society outwardly by controlling education
and all the means of production, but underneath the
imposing façade to leave things essentially unchanged.
Christian revolution, as distinct from communist
revolution, claims that human nature must be changed
from within, otherwise the same old problems will
continue to reassert themselves. It is not enough to
rearrange the scenery on the stage. We must also
improve the play and change the character of the
actors. To put it another way, Christian revolution
begins in the deep secret places of personality, but it
spreads till it permeates the entire fabric of society. It
is not possible to understand what Jesus had in mind
when he expounded this parable until we give full
value to the words "till the whole was leavened".

One last thing—this parable reminds us that only a
living faith is contagious. There is nothing static about
yeast; it bubbles and seethes and ferments. Beginning

at the centre, its influence reaches out to the circumference. Never quiescent, it acts vigorously till the whole lump is leavened. Similarly, with a living faith, it has yeast-like properties and it propagates itself by the infection of an inexpressible exuberance.

"Religion," said Dean Inge, "is not so much taught as caught". "One loving heart," said the great Augustine, "sets another on fire," and he was doubtless talking from personal experience. When first he heard Bishop Ambrose preach, this brilliant young professor was most critical and felt very superior. The presentation of the message is faulty and the sermons are full of logical inconsistencies, thought Augustine; but, critical as he felt, he could not stay away. Ambrose drew him like a magnet, and at last he fell under his spell which later on led to his conversion in the orchard.

Here, surely, we touch the inner nerve of the Church's failure and ineffectiveness. There are over a million and a quarter members of the Church of Scotland, and each one is supposed to be a live cell spreading the contagion of the faith throughout the land. A million and a quarter live cells! What a revolutionary ferment they could create if only they were alive and active and potent!

In the end it comes down to very simple fact—you cannot transmit enthusiasm unless you have it, nor can you communicate a living faith to others till first you are able to say with Jeremiah, "But his word was in mine heart as a burning fire shut up in my bones." We are ineffective, because our faith is formal, not vital, a matter of outer conformity, not of inner conviction,

G

traditional acquiescence, not personal apprehension. How can we stab the masses awake out of their slumbering indifference? Only when we possess a faith which acts like leaven, potent, contagious, irresistible.

SECTION III

DOCTRINAL

INTRODUCTION

It is commonly believed that theology is the preserve of professionals, while preaching is the preoccupation of ordinary ministers who endeavour to communicate the Christian message as skilfully and persuasively as they know how. This is not merely a false, but a fatal dichotomy, and a Church that comes to terms with it is already under sentence of death.

The subject matter of theology is the revelation of God in history reaching fulness and absolute finality in Jesus Christ. This also is the subject-matter of preaching, therefore it is not possible to divorce the two without doing irreparable damage to the christian faith. They both have a supreme loyalty to one momentous event and there can be no separation.

Whether the claim that theology can be considered as science is true or not, we would all concede that to do justice to its subject-matter it must have a technical language. The task of the preacher is to take the insights of theology and to express them in an idiom which the average man can understand. This is not easy. The preacher's function is to communicate the message not merely to the spiritual *élite* and to those who sympathise, but to the mass of his contemporaries. If he does not consider communication as a matter of supreme importance, it is questionable whether he takes seriously the content of the message he is commissioned to declare.

AND HE WAS MADE MAN

"And they feared exceedingly, and said one to another, What manner of man is this, that even the wind and the sea obey him?"

St. Mark 4, 41

THERE is one fact which Christian theology has consistently asserted and it is this, "Jesus was a real man". In the first and second centuries the Church had to fight a school of heretics called Docetists. And why did they get into trouble? Our natural reaction is to suppose that they denied the Divinity of Christ, but oddly enough the truth happens to be the opposite. It never occurred to them to question His Deity, but they did declare that He only appeared to suffer and that He was not fully human. There are perhaps no Docetists in our midst today, but there are many Christians who have the uneasy feeling that if they stress Christ's humanity they are in the very act subtracting from His Divinity. Nothing could be further from the truth. This form of spiritual astigmatism must be corrected at all costs.

The New Testament makes it clear that Jesus was no demi-god, no celestial Titan masquerading in human shape, but a real man. Physically, He was human. There were times when He was exhausted, and the gospels frankly record that on His way to Calvary He staggered and fell to the ground under the weight of His own Cross. Emotionally, He was human. He knew the meaning of anger; He experienced moments of joy and sorrow like the rest of us; and the tears He shed at the grave of Lazarus were not sham tears. Mentally, He was human. In many respects He was a child of His own times and, while His insights were uncanny, He had to make do with the limitation of knowledge which is a badge of our mortality. The Gospels leave us with the indelible impression that whatever else Jesus was, He was a real man—bone of our bone and flesh of our flesh.

This is of crucial importance. If Jesus was not human in every sense of the word, it means that He has no real kinship with us, and therefore He cannot speak to our condition. Furthermore, it means that God did not take our human predicament seriously. If God did not come all the way to meet us, if He did not descend into the arena of our need, there is no solving of our problem, no healing of our malaise, no release from our bondage, and the word salvation is drained of all meaning.

But we cannot leave the matter there. When we say that Jesus was a man, indeed the greatest of all men, we know we have not adequately described Him. Whatever the crisis—a storm at sea, a verbal duel with His enemies, the agony of Gethsemane, the slow, savage death by crucifixion—He was master of the situation. He possessed a mysterious quality which evades our grasp and defies our analysis. Like His own disciples, we feel there are immensities and depths in Him we do not even begin to understand, so we too are compelled to ask, "What manner of man is this?"

Consider how this question is thrust on us by His teaching. There have been eminent philosophers who have propounded their own brand of ethics—Plato, Aristotle and Spinoza, to mention only a few—but in comparison with Jesus the impact of their thinking has been on the whole conspicuously unimpressive. But here is an untutored village carpenter, who, as far as we know, did not even commit His thoughts to paper, yet individuals and nations some twenty centuries after His death, stand judged in the light of His pronouncements. His teaching digs us out of the snug burrows of our habitual complacency. It has an astringent quality about it which hurts before it begins to heal.

There is its penetration. It pierced through man's defences and subtle sophistries right to the inner marrow of his being. We talk of depth psychology today, of the need to probe deep down beneath the surface to the essential core of things, but Jesus practised this in Galilee long ago. Here are a few examples: "A man's life consisteth not in the abundance of the things which he possesseth." "No man can serve two masters." "Which of you by taking thought can add one cubit unto his stature?" "Whosoever shall seek to save his life shall lose it: and whosoever shall lose his life shall preserve it." These insights of Jesus are not only penetrating and profound, they are also timeless, as apposite today as when they were first spoken.

Again there is its originality. Those who go out of their way to rob Jesus of His Divine stature, claim that there is nothing in His teaching which cannot be found in most of the other higher religions. This is a false assessment. Judged by any standard, Jesus was a daring innovator. He was a spiritual Columbus sailing into uncharted seas, an intrepid explorer mapping out continents of thought never before examined. His originality consisted not in discovering brand new ideas, but in taking traditional ones and giving them a fresh meaning and significance. Others before Him had described God as Father, but what Jesus did was to take a belief that at best hovered around the circumference of man's thinking and place it at the centre. He made it the hub from which the spokes of everything in heaven and earth radiated out, the axis round which the entire universe revolved.

Then there is its authority. The way he finishes the Sermon on the Mount is simply breath-taking: "Therefore whosoever heareth these sayings of mine, and doeth them, I will liken him unto a wise man, which built his house upon a rock: And the rain descended, and the floods came, and the winds blew, and beat upon that house; and it fell not: for it was founded upon a rock." And when a man sick with palsy was brought to Him, He said, "Son, thy sins be forgiven thee." The God Jesus speaks of is not a bloodless abstraction, but a real Being from whose challenge there is no escape. Who then is this who authoritatively proclaims the gospel of forgiveness, and actually exercises a prerogative which belongs to God alone? What manner of man is this? So much for His teaching.

Consider again how this question is thrust upon us

by His personality. When Sir William Orpen was painting the portrait of Cosmo Gordon Lang, the former Archbishop of Canterbury, he asked, "I see seven archbishops. Which am I to paint?" Anyone who naïvely supposes he can draw a simple portrait of the Christ of the Gospels is sadly mistaken. Not only is a historical photograph out of the question, but the kind of biographical portrait Boswell drew of Johnson, based on actual reminiscence and full of intensely interesting details, is also doomed to failure. The personality that emerges so powerfully from the Gospels is one that is full of sharp contradictions.

Jesus combined an intense spirituality with a robust earthiness. Prayer to Him was the breath of life and He was perfectly attuned to the unseen world that lies beyond the senses, but at the same time He revelled in the sights and sounds of nature, in the wind that blows and the rain that descends, in the harvest that ripens and the sparrow that falls to the ground.

Jesus also combined a striking humility with a startling consciousness of His own uniqueness. Here is a humility of which the manger cradle is the initial symbol, and the Cross, bleak upon the hill, the inevitable climax. He who said that He was meek and lowly of heart did not hesitate to speak and act for God. The pronoun "I" is very prominent in His teaching and He makes staggering and stupendous claims for Himself. Familiarity no doubt has dulled our ears, but to those who first heard them, they must have sounded like detonating bombs.

Again, Jesus combined a love as broad and deep as

life itself with an anger that at times rose up within Him like a river bursting its banks. His love reached out and reclaimed the lost, and in the final extremity of physical agony on the Cross, it embraced even his executioners. "Father forgive them for they know not what they do". Yet His anger was terrible to behold when He lashed the scribes and Pharisees with savage eloquence and drove the money-changers out of the Temple.

All this is true, but at the end of the day the impression Jesus leaves with us is one not of contradiction, but of integration. Virtues which in others show separately are in Him strangely coalesced and blended. He is never deflected from His purpose by the applause of the crowd, the flattery of His friends or the machinations of His enemies. He is always sure of Himself and His mastery over every crisis belongs to the category of miracle. The most astonishing fact in the New Testament is not this or that miracle, but the personality that inspires its pages and dominates it from beginning to end. Like His own bewildered disciples we too can only ask, "What manner of man is this?"

Finally, consider how this question is thrust on us by the fact of Christian experience. The New Testament gives us an account of His teaching, and a portrait of His personality, but it also records the impressions of men who had experienced His risen, living presence. They marched out into a cruel world armed not with a fashionable philosophy or a controversial theology, but with the burning conviction that Jesus, having defeated evil and death, was Lord of all life. We find no trace of ambiguity in the testimony of the Emmaus road disciples, "Did not our heart burn within us while he talked with us by the way?" And Paul could not be more explicit, "I live: yet not I, but Christ liveth in me."

To those who advance the theory that religious experience belongs entirely to the realm of subjective fancy, we could, I daresay, retort that the argument is ambivalent. What guarantee have we that the proponents of such a theory are not themselves victims of wish fulfilment? We are on more solid ground, however, when we are able to point to men, noted for superior commonsense, intellectual brilliance, and balanced, integrated personalities, who have reiterated a thousand times over that Jesus is a living reality as well as a historical fact. Augustine had a fairly large dose of scepticism in his make-up; so had Pascal, William Temple and C. S. Lewis; yet agonisingly they came to believe that Jesus was an eternal contemporary. It would be arrogant to dismiss such a claim as irrelevant, especially when it is made by men of integrity, and by men who, acting on the basis of this conviction, have changed history.

Since the Incarnation is nothing other than the coming of the Kingdom of God among men, Christian experience is never a private affair. It is only meaningful within the community of all those whom God has called. Just as no single instrument can begin to perform a symphony, or do justice to the intention of the composer, so no individual, however real his experience of God, can convey the full meaning of the divine purpose as it is revealed in Christ. A Christian understanding of God requires the glorious company of the apostles, the goodly fellowship of the prophets, the noble army of martyrs, the Holy Church throughout all the world.

What manner of man is this? This was the question which the panic-stricken disciples posed in their perplexity. Even with two thousand years of Christian tradition behind us, we do not claim to have explained the mystery, for mystery it will remain to the end of time, but as Christians we do affirm that Jesus was both man and God. This conviction carries with it fearful and far-reaching consequences. If it is true that God Himself became involved in the human predicament, then it follows that men can no longer be neutral. Already they have said yes or no to this question and His own words take on a new meaning: "He that is not with me is against me, and he that does not gather with me, scattereth." Matt 12³⁰

2

WHAT THE CROSS NAILS DOWN

"Blotting out the handwriting of ordinances that was against us, which was contrary to us, and took it out of the way, nailing it to his cross;

And having spoiled principalities and powers, he made a shew of them openly, triumphing over them in it."

Colossians 2, 14–15

WHEN we grapple with profound mysteries we have to use metaphor and images to make ourselves understood. This is precisely what Paul is doing when, writing to the Christians at Colossae, he endeavours to expound the doctrine of the Atonement. He uses two or three images, which, in his eagerness to convey to them the essential meaning of the Cross, he somehow or other manages to mix up. One is that of a champion who comes to our rescue when we are under sentence of death. He saves us by the simple expedient of taking the charge under which we stand condemned, and blotting out the fatal writing. Another image he uses refers to an ancient custom which cancelled a debt by driving a nail through a document placarded at some conspicuous place like a street corner or market square. Or perhaps Paul had in mind the practice of suspending above the head of the victim the charge on which he was condemned, such as the superscription, "THIS IS THE KING OF THE JEWS". So Jesus by his atoning death cancels out all our liabilities, and this guarantee we see written out by the hand of God Himself upon the Cross.

No wonder Paul gets his images mixed up, for he is speaking about the Cross standing at the heart of our faith and providing it with its characteristic symbol. He is trying to express the inexpressible, to explain something significant beyond our understanding, pointing to heights towering beyond our human reach and to depths of meaning we can never hope to plumb.

Even the great classical theories of the Atonement fail to do justice to the fact of the Cross. Anselm, who claims that God's holiness and honour demanded the sacrifice of Jesus as the only means of reconciliation, no doubt got hold of a very important aspect of the truth, but it was by no means the whole truth. The same thing can be said of Abelard whose name is associated with the Moral Theory, which claims that only by means of the Cross can man believe in and respond to the love of God. The third theory, revived and expounded by Bishop Aulen in his book *Christus Victor*, published in 1931, asserts that the Atonement from start to finish is a cosmic but victorious conflict between God on the one hand and the concentrated might of the forces of evil on the other. But it vindicates this claim at the cost of soft-pedalling the other two conceptions which however inadequate they may be in themselves surely belong to the total understanding of the Cross. A contemporary American theologian[1] who would go so far as to reject the traditional theories of the Atonement, nevertheless admits that the Cross

[1] Professor John Knox, Union Theological Seminary, New York.

plays havoc with all our theological systems and leaves us at the end of the day face to face with a mystery which we can never hope to unravel. He writes, "The stake on Calvary points in two directions—to abominable depths of evil which we can never measure with our science or restrain with our rules, and to a goodness as far above us as the skies . . . Accepting the Cross does not mean understanding it, it means almost the contrary—recognising a dimension and a potency in human life which defy our comprehension and all our little systems whether of law or truth."

It is fatally easy to discuss the Cross as a theological abstraction which permits of conflicting theories and different interpretations, and in so doing to lose sight of its inner meaning and poignant challenge. To the Christian martyrs of the first century, who experienced the sadistic fury of Nero and were put to death with exquisite cruelty, the Cross was no mere academic issue—but the fount of their inspiration and the unfailing reservoir from which they drew their superhuman courage. Paul, while he was desperately interested in working out its theological implications, was never guilty of preaching it as an academic abstraction. On the contrary, he would claim that there are certain concrete realities which the Cross nails down for us, from which there is no possible escape.

One fact which the cross nails down is *the grim reality of sin*. Even the Pharisees, puritans though they were, did not take sin sufficiently seriously. They recognised it, of course, as one of the brute facts of life, and they imagined its grip could be broken by ritual sacrifice

H

and correct ceremonial practices. But their facile panaceas proved impotent before this stubborn malaise and they underestimated the demonic quality of the enemy they had to contend with.

This has been an ever-recurring temptation, and the Victorians were notoriously guilty of it. In the absence of major global conflicts they convinced themselves that progress was not only inevitable, but also divinely predestinated. The atmosphere, men like Herbert Spencer and Robert Browning breathed, vibrated with a false sense of cheerful harmony. Evolution and science and fashionable philosophies were baptised with bubbling optimism, and Utopia was believed to be just around the corner.

Today those who march against the bomb and tremble under an atomic sword of Damocles are no longer starry-eyed about universal happiness, but the seriousness of the time does not prevent them from flirting with plans which are prepared to reckon with everything except the reality of evil. In his recent book, Sir Julian Huxley once again voices this naïve humanistic optimism. He argues that without recourse to any God or any supernatural aid, man is the measure of all things if only he will draw wisely on the resources which are latent within his own personality.

Isn't this precisely the lie which Jesus nailed down on Calvary? The Cross if it demonstrates anything at all, declares that sin is not the shadow cast by the good, nor is it inertia or ignorance which we can dispel by exercising our native ingenuity. It ridicules the common notion that once you educate people and teach a right sense of values, they will act accordingly. Caiaphas, the high priest, was no ignoramus. Herod was not an uncultured boor and Pilate was no untutored savage; yet they were the principal agents in the drama of the Crucifixion and between them they perpetrated the most shocking crime in history.

Can our sentimental philosophies about man's essential goodness stand up to the scorching light of the Cross? Can we still confidently say, "Give him a chance and I wager he'll give a good account of himself." Well he had his chance the day Pilate cried, "Whom will ye that I release unto you, Barabbas or Jesus which is called Christ?" And what did man do? He cold-bloodedly decided for Barabbas and clamoured for the destruction of Christ. The Cross shatters our fond illusions about man and reveals the full measure of his sinfulness and the unplumbed depth of his sadistic wickedness. It stands there on the gaunt hill outside the city walls as a symbol of our stupidity, our criminal blindness, or insatiable cruelty.

Another fact which the cross nails down is *the agonising cost of forgiveness.* What we commonly call the Atonement has puzzled Christians from the beginning, and to the modern man nothing is more uncongenial and unintelligible. "If God loves us," he argues, "and if Jesus gave us a true picture of His character in the parable of the Prodigal Son, then why the Cross?" If it is true, as the New Testament claims, that God, instead of waiting till His honour was satisfied, actually took the initiative and set out to save men while they were denying His existence and defying His holy will, in what sense then can we talk meaningfully of the Atonement?

One thing at least is certain, when a man takes sin seriously he finds it desperately hard to forgive. When we hear of someone saying forgiveness is easy, we can be sure he is not forgiving sin, but only condoning it, and that is another matter altogether. The reprehensible practice, becoming fashionable of late, of divorced couples proclaiming their mutual affection from the house-tops and even holidaying together does not spring from Christian charity. The honest man knows that to condone sin is easy, but to forgive it is hard. And that for two reasons.

One is that if we value anything highly, we bitterly resent whatever seeks to harm or destroy it. In Galsworthy's *Forsyte Saga* Soames, the man of property, is depicted as a cold-blooded, rather timid, comfort-loving materialist. Possessed of a unique flair for amassing money, he is also a connoisseur of art. Over the years he collected a number of masterpieces which he hung in a gallery at the top of the house, and from time to time he used to enter and gaze at them in rapt admiration. One day fire broke out, raging through the priceless pictures; and Soames, no longer timid, beat back the licking flames with his bare hands, and in his effort to save what he really cared for he perished.

The other is that it is extremely hard to forgive those whom we love and who have disgraced us. If we see a drunk person staggering down the street, bumping into people and behaving oddly, we smile as a rule, and even philosophise on the likable traits possessed by many drunkards. But if the person concerned happens to be your husband or your son, your wife or your daughter, how very different. You don't smile tolerantly: you resent it bitterly, and to forgive, you need a large measure of the grace of God.

This may help us to understand how hard it was for Christ to forgive. No one ever took sin so seriously and no one ever loved people with such a holy passion. In His eyes the individual was of an infinite value—a masterpiece—a unique original for which there was no substitute. Considering how much He hated sin, the miracle is that He loved the sinner. But at what a cost! Forgiveness, if it is genuine, always means self-substitution; therefore the Cross is not an ingenious conundrum thought up by theologians—its shaft sinks deep into the meaning of life. It declares that, in Christ, God Himself suffered and atoned for our sins. The Cross is the measure of what it cost Him to forgive us.

There is one more fact which the Cross nails down. It is *the victorious purpose of God.* This message belongs to the warp and woof of the New Testament. Paul in the words he addresses to the Colossians gives it a particularly arresting expression. The picture he paints is not that of the pale emaciated Christ, beloved of medieval artists, hanging supinely on a cross, nor of a lamb led to the slaughter by those who had cunningly engineered His death, nor of one who was the plaything of circumstances beyond His control, much less of one who was annihilated because He had run foul of tradition and the deeply entrenched forces of the Establishment. On the contrary, the Christ of this letter is one who launched the offensive against his enemies, who, far from meekly acquiescing in anything, is engaged in blotting things out, nailing things down, sabotaging the schemes of evil men, triumphing over principalities and powers.

Think for a moment of the miracle of the Cross. Two thousand years after the event, millions of people come together to celebrate the most colossal failure in history. For make no mistake about it, judged by our normal criteria of success, Jesus had definitely failed. In Jerusalem He had appealed for a reform of religion and His reward was crucifixion. Even those He trained to form the spearhead of His Church in the hour of crisis forsook Him and fled. On Good Friday, from whatever angle we care to view it, the mission of Jesus looked like a complete and irrevocable failure. Yet this is the strange and challenging paradox—the most tragic of all defeats turned out to be the greatest triumph of righteousness ever won.

It is easy for us to be wise some twenty centuries after it all happened, but how did Jesus see it from the beginning? How did He know that to fail was the surest way to succeed? What a sense of mastery He conveys as He stands at the heart of the cosmic drama where good and evil are locked in desperate struggle, striving for supremacy. We get the impression that it is Herod, Pilate and Caiaphas—convinced they are in control of events, and not this helpless peasant on the Cross—who are the real pawns of circumstance. It is easy for us to see it now, but Jesus saw it in the hour of calamity, apparently crushing and irreversible. Even then He saw that the victory was His and the power and the glory.

In Paul's thinking, the Cross and its atoning work is only meaningful in the light of the Resurrection. "Christ being raised from the dead, dieth no more; death has no dominion over Him." The Cross is a manifestation, not of the weakness but of the power of God. It is a symbol not only of the eternal love that never lets us go, but also of the victorious purpose of God, running through all creation and all history from the beginning, till that day when the kingdoms of this world are become the Kingdom of our Lord and of His Christ and He shall reign for ever and ever.

More than once I have gone to the Glasgow Art Galleries to see Dali's painting of the Crucifixion. I don't know what precisely the artist had in mind, but the message he manages to convey to me is a fortifying one. Dali's Christ is looking down from a great height upon the world. But what rivets attention straight away is the powerful muscles and broad shoulders. This is not the limp, pain-drenched figure of the traditional crucifix. This is someone who reigns from the Cross—the Christ whom the New Testament describes as the "KING OF KINGS AND LORD OF LORDS."

3

THE SIGNIFICANCE OF THE
RESURRECTION

"For I delivered unto you first of all that which I also received, how that Christ died for our sins according to the scriptures;

And that he was buried, and that he rose again the third day according to the scriptures;

And that he was seen of Cephas, then of the twelve:

After that, he was seen of above five hundred brethren at once; of whom the greater part remain unto this present, but some are fallen asleep.

After that, he was seen of James; then of all the apostles.

And last of all he was seen of me also, as of one born out of due time."

I Corinthians 15, 3–8

RUNNING through all Tennessee Williams' plays there is one basic theme—the reality of death. It is possible to wrap ourselves round with all sorts of warm and comforting illusions and to anaesthetise our inner anxiety with exciting pleasures and titillating distractions, argues Williams, but in the end we cannot evade this brute fact of our terrestrial existence. Death waits for everyman, mocking all his dreams and wantonly destroying what he holds most dear in life—love itself.

Death obtrudes everywhere, not only in the mounting

carnage on the roads, not only in the increasing number of victims claimed by coronary thrombosis and cancer, but also in the imminent threat of an atomic holocaust. The fear of death is the basic anxiety, declares Paul Tillich, and perhaps our nervous disorders and our frantic pursuit of pleasure stem from our reluctance to come to terms with it as an enemy we must all reckon with.

Tennessee Williams takes death seriously and, being an agnostic, he tries to face its grim inexorable finality with the defiant courage of a stoic. The Bible also takes death seriously—it calls it the last enemy, and even goes so far as to claim that finite history, however meaningful it may appear to be, can have no permanence. We look in vain for the self-conscious realism which characterises so much of modern literature. This book, which oddly enough remains a best seller in an age of secularism, boldly faces this grim enigma and proclaims its answer in the Ressurrection of Jesus Christ from the dead.

H. G. Wells contemptuously dismisses the Resurrection as "a nice epilogue, a happy ending imposed by a sentimental editor on an essentially tragic novel or play." This only goes to show that Wells either did not read the New Testament, or if he did, failed to understand it. The Ressurrection is not a happy ending to a sad story. Nor is it the climax of the gospel, in the sense that prior to it there was a gospel able to stand on its own feet. That is not how the first disciples understood the Resurrection, and that is not how they preached it. For them there was no gospel apart from the Resurrection. It is both arrogant and impious of anyone to speak of a gospel which is distinct from the Resurrection, for the all-sufficient reason that those who wrote the New Testament were men who acknowledged the crucified Jesus as the living Lord and proclaimed that God had raised Him from the dead.

What we have to grasp is that the Ressurrection is not a lovely after-thought, an explanatory addendum, a mere epilogue, tagged on to the main story about Jesus. It stands at the centre of the faith as the axis round which Christianity revolves. The God Christians believe in is essentially the Resurrection God. When Peter says, "Blessed be God the Father of our Lord Jesus Christ who hath begotten us again unto a lively hope by the Resurrection of Jesus Christ from the dead," he is speaking for his fellow-apostles and for the whole of the New Testament. The fact of the Resurrection is rooted both in history and theology.

To begin with let us consider the *historical evidence*. The earliest documentary evidence at our disposal in favour of the Resurrection is found in the first Epistle of Paul to the Corinthians, Chapter 15. Paul, writing to fellow-Christians at Corinth round about A.D. 55, reminds them of the tradition passed on to him after his own conversion. According to scholars, he is here repeating a fixed formula which dates back to the first decade after the crucifixion.

In this important passage Paul names three individuals and three groups to whom Christ had appeared. The first individual was Cephas, or Peter, whom Paul had visited in Jerusalem for fifteen days, and who had presumably given him a first-hand report. The second individual was James, the brother of our Lord, whom Paul had met during the same visit; and who, according to the gospel of John, was a sceptic till the Resurrection. The third was Paul himself; thus we have a direct statement from one who saw the risen Christ: "And last of all He was seen of me also as of one born out of due time." The three groups to whom Christ appeared were the Twelve, all the Apostles, and a body of more than five hundred believers. They could hardly have been the victims of mass psychology; in that case we would expect the experiences to spread more and more, whereas here they are strictly limited.

The evidence of Paul is supplemented by the Evangelist's accounts of Jesus's appearances to the disciples and by their testimony to the empty tomb. Indeed we are left with the strong impression that no gospel or epistle would ever have been written if the Resurrection had not taken place. Professor James Denny hits the nail on the head when he says, "It is not the story of the empty Tomb or the appearing of Jesus in Jerusalem or in Galilee which is the primary evidence of the Resurrection—it is the New Testament itself."

Again, there is the evidence provided by the existence of the Christian Church. What happened so to change the disillusioned survivors of a lost cause into reckless crusaders calling upon a brutal world to repent and be baptised? This question, which puzzled the religious leaders of that day, demands an honest answer. Still as sharp, insistent and imperious as ever, it is not possible for the historian to side-step it.

If the historian suggests that the Resurrection was but the projection of the disciples' inner hopes, how does he explain the fact that the Resurrection took them by surprise, shattering their presuppositions and stretching them far beyond themselves. If, on the other hand, he claims that the first disciples were so dominated by the personality of Jesus that they refused to believe that He was dead, how does he account for the curious fact that the centre of the Apostolic preaching was not the personality of Jesus, but the Cross and the Resurrection?

Furthermore, the historian is left with the rather awkward task of explaining not only the emergence but also the continued existence of the Church. By all the laws of probability, Nero and Domitan should have destroyed her. Persecution from without and corruption from within should have long since laid her in her grave. But despite the fury of her enemies and the treachery of her professed representatives, the Church has survived, and for this miracle there is only one satisfying explanation—the indwelling Presence of the Risen, Living Lord.

The historical evidence in favour of the Resurrection is strong, but by itself it will not create the certainty which characterises a believing Christian. The evidence may lead us, as it led Frank Morrison, to question and to discard our own presuppositions, but it will not make us cry, "My Lord and my God". The evidence is impressive, but it is not scientific proof, and it is no use pretending that it is. At the end of the day the acceptance of the Resurrection springs not from a study of

"Who moved the Stone?"

the evidence, but from an act of faith.

We have considered the historical evidence of the Resurrection. Let us now consider its *theological significance*. The Resurrection confirms our belief in the Divinity of Christ. There is a sense in which the most thorough-going sceptic will agree that Jesus was unique. He was unique as a teacher of ethics: He was unique as a literary artist, a master of the short story and immortal epigram. His is unique in the place He has carved for Himself in history and the influence He has exerted on the thinking of mankind. All this the sceptic concedes, but further than that he will not go. On the other hand, Christian orthodoxy, while acknowledging the uniqueness of Jesus on a human level, affirms that He was unique in a more absolute sense—in that He was none other than God incarnate in human flesh.

From the very start, the disciples knew that Jesus was no ordinary man. He spoke as no one else spoke and his personality exercised a magnetic spell and exuded a mysterious power. All this they recognised, but they did not proclaim His Divinity with passionate certainty till after His Resurrection. With their doubts banished and their fumblings finished, the note that sounds forth is clear and unmistakable, "This Jesus whom we preach is not a mere man, but God Himself come to visit and redeem His people." As then, so now. The acceptance of the Resurrection silences any doubt about Christ's Divinity. The Christ who rose in triumph from the grave bursts through all our human categories, and the absolutely unique relationship in which He stands with God is what we mean by His Deity.

Another belief that the Resurrection confirms for us is the Righteousness of God. Sartre is not only an eminent philosopher, he is also a brilliant novelist and playwright. And whatever the medium he uses, he has only one message — the meaninglessness of the universe, rendering our individual existence a trivial and pointless business. Sartre and his fellow-writers, while they declare there is no such thing as cosmic righteousness, concede that life sometimes forces us to behave as if there were. This only deepens the irony of the human situation.

We are living in a crassly cynical age characterised by international lawlessness, increasing crime, and an eruption of violence among youth not only in the democratic countries, but also in Soviet Russia. No doubt this is a complex problem defying a simple, straightforward analysis, but behind it all lies this sense of meaninglessness, confusing our values and sapping our vital energies. How can we expect people to behave sanely and to think constructively if they believe that Whirl is King and that Chance sits upon the throne of the universe?

But Christians are committed to believe that Sartre and those who think as he does are wrong, to think that they are the victims of fate, or the playthings of circumstance. And the pivot of their faith is the Resurrection of Jesus Christ from the dead. At Calvary evil launched its most savage attack: there the forces of darkness organised themselves against the Lord and his anointed, crying, "Let us break their bands asunder and cast their cords from us," but God vindicated His invincible purpose when He raised Jesus from the dead. The Resurrection, correctly understood, is far more than the reanimation of someone dead and buried: it declares that God is in supreme control and that wickedness will never win.

One last thing. The Resurrection adds a new dimension to our belief in the after life. Here we must differentiate a general belief in the immortality of the soul from what is specifically Christian doctrine. Since the time of Plato, the Hellenistic world had been familiar with the former. Apart from the difficulty of conceiving how a disembodied soul can exist, this doctrine is suspect because the self as we know it is far more than a naked soul, and without some form of bodily expression we cannot say that the complete self survives. A man is not a soul—he is, to use the common jargon, a psycho-somatic unity—and that is the truth the Apostles' Creed preserves when it talks of the Resurrection of the Body. This does not imply the resurrection of bones and muscles and the revivification of our flesh, but it does imply the raising of the complete self into newness of life.

This basic point has been well expressed in modern terms by Dr. A. M. Ramsay, the present Archbishop of Canterbury: "To abandon the use of the word 'body' in connection with the Resurrection of the dead would indeed remove certain difficulties. But it would introduce difficulties no less great, and it would involve us in the poverty and materialism of limiting the word 'body' to the body as we know it in its earthly and frustrated state. To cling to the words 'the Resurrection of the body' is to affirm that in our present bodies there is the law of a bodily life beyond our dreams, when the Spirit of Him who raised up Jesus Christ has done His perfect work in us."

4

THE BIBLE AND
THE HUMAN PREDICAMENT

"And the priest said, The sword of Goliath the
Philistine, whom thou slewest in the valley of Elah,
behold, it is here wrapped in a cloth behind the
ephod: if thou wilt take that, take it: for there is no
other save that here. And David said, There is none
like that; give it to me."

I Samuel 21, 9

THIS is one of those dramatic stories which so often leap
out at us from the Old Testament. David, on a desperate
mission, found himself hungry and defenceless. After
eating the shewbread from off the altar, he looked
round for a suitable weapon. "There is none," replied
the priest, "except the sword of Goliath which you see
wrapped up in a cloth behind the ephod." David,
remembering the unequal contest of his youth and his
incredible victory, cried out in enthusiasm, "Give it
to me, there is none like it."

There is a sense in which we can compare the Bible
with the sword of Goliath, a mighty weapon forged for
a definite purpose, yet lying idly on show, a sacred
symbol of battles long ago and far away. No one can
doubt the veneration in which the Bible is universally
held. Translated into no fewer than 1,100 languages,
well over 20,000,000 copies of it are sold every year

throughout the world. Every time a witness is cross-examined in court, he has to swear on the Bible that he will tell the truth, the whole truth and nothing but the truth. In the Coronation service, seen by thousands crushed into Westminster Abbey, and by millions viewing it on television, one of the most moving scenes was where the Moderator of the General Assembly of the Church of Scotland handed the Bible to the newly-crowned Queen with the words, "Here is wisdom. This is the Royal Law. These are the lively oracles of God."

These facts are very impressive, but we must not allow ourselves to be deceived by them. The truth is that though we pay considerable lip service to the Bible, we are not inclined to mould our lives on its teachings. We regard it as a quaint hang-over from a more credulous past, as something which achieves the rather unique distinction of being a best-seller, yet which few seem to read. In short, the Bible may have been a mighty weapon in times past, but now it is no more than a museum specimen, a national trophy — a sacred relic wrapped up in the wrong kind of reverence.

We are celebrating the 350th anniversary of the Authorised Version and it is only right that we should recognise this great landmark in the literary and religious life of Britain. Its influence on our thoughts and speech is simply incalculable. The poetry of men like T. S. Eliot and Dylan Thomas is steeped in its idiom, and the verbal images of a dramatist like John Osborne are strongly conditioned by it. But perhaps in its very beauty and the extent of its cultural influenc lies the Authorised Version's greatest potential danger. For most people it has become a sword of Goliath, wrapped in memorable phrases and haunting cadences, which blunt the sharp edge of its challenge. They forget that the language is merely incidental: it is the message wrapped up in it that is so important. After all, the written word is only meaningful when it bears witness to the living word that speaks through it.

Therefore, we must welcome the New English Bible with anticipation and eagerness. Since 1611, Biblical scholarship has increased immeasurably in range and accuracy. In the interval, thousands of manuscripts, documents and fragments of various sizes, of different degrees of importance have been discovered in monasteries or reclaimed by archaeologists from excavations, or from the rubbish dumps of cities. It is both stupid and impious to invest the Authorised Version with absolute infallibility and to dismiss all new translations in the words of the inveterate traditionalist who once remarked, "If the Authorised Version was good enough for St. Paul, it is good enough for me." We are greatly indebted to modern Biblical scholarship and in particular at this time, to those men who over a period of years have devoted themselves to this rewarding task.

If the Bible is to recover for us its lost meaning and potency, if it is to cease being an ancient relic wrapped up in all sorts of protective coverings, if it is to speak once again with shattering relevance to our condition, then we must shed many of our cast-iron prejudices and preconceived notions and approach it with intelligence as well as reverence. We must not go to the

Bible looking for the wrong kind of information.

We must not regard it as a scientific text-book.

Scientists today are exercised by two intriguing questions—how the Universe began and how man evolved from lowly origins. The sceptic feels he has demolished the Bible with one blow, by claiming it throws no light on these issues. This is a mistaken notion, for the Bible is not really interested in the scientific details of origins, but in the much more important question of why things came into existence. Nothing that either Hoyle or Ryle of Cambridge can say about the nature of the Universe, can cancel out the claim of the Book of Genesis "In the beginning— God".

We must not regard it as a historical text-book.

That is not to say that the Bible is not rooted and grounded in history. It most assuredly is, covering a period ranging from 2,000 B.C. to A.D. 100. It tells us many interesting things about nomad tribes, Egyptian Pharaohs, Assyrian dictators, puppet kings and the rise and fall of Empires. While a great deal of the information it gives us has been corroborated by archaeological research, the Bible is more interested in demonstrating selected events which show the hand of God in His actions with men than in cataloguing facts.

We must not regard it as a conventional biography.

It incidentally supplies us with a great deal of useful information about figures like Jeremiah, Moses, Paul and even Jesus Himself. But it leaves a great deal to our imaginations. It doesn't tell us what Jesus looked like, how He was educated, whether He was a good carpenter or not. You search the New Testament in vain for that sort of biographical tittle-tattle you meet in Boswell's Johnson. This is so, because the aim of the Bible is basically not historical, but theological. Personality traits are interesting only in so far as they throw a light on the nautre of man and the nature of God.

The Bible is absolutely unique in that it is neither a code of ethical maxims, nor a compendium of religious truisms. Though it is immensely interested in the future and says many strong things about the Eternal Hope, it really describes how God has acted in history and draws our attention to what has already taken place once and for all. The Bible must be examined and sifted and translated from time to time in the light of newly acquired knowledge, but it can never be superseded. It stands at the heart of Christian thought and Christian worship. It is the Word of God because it speaks to our condition today and will continue to do so world without end.

This Book is irreplaceable because it gives us *an analysis of the human predicament*. That there is a desperate predicament, not even the most blasé optimist is prepared to deny. Even men who are self-professed sceptics, have of late joined the ranks of the prophets and are heard crying to a world bent on its own destruction, "Repent or perish". Bertrand Russell has jettisoned his reputation as a dispassionate, detached philosopher, a cold-blooded analyst of the human

situation—and has become a flaming crusader, proclaiming a programme of survival for the race, ere it
is too late.

Most of us are prepared to concede this, but many
are still inclined to attribute our problems to causes
which can be eradicated by human planning and
heroic endeavour. There are those who with Karl
Marx cling to the social theory of evil. They argue that
the root of our trouble is the scandal of social inequality;
eliminate that and the promised land is just round the
next corner. There are others who sponsor the "evolu-
tionary lag" theory. Man, geologically speaking, has
only just emerged from the primeval forest and it will
take him a long time to shake off his animal heritage.
Finally, there is the theory which equates evil with
igonrance and regards knowledge, especially of the
scientific variety, as the one and only saviour.

All these theories have one weakness in common—
a failure to face up to the seriousness of the human
predicament. They must stand self-conscious and
acutely embarrassed before brutal facts that bombard
us today from all sides. In an age of affluence, crime and
juvenile delinquency are on the increase. In an age of
ever-widening educational facilities, moral restraint is
becoming a relic of the past, and in an age in which
the psychologist is the high priest of society, nervous
and mental disorders are more prevalent than ever
before. Professor Jung contemptuously dismisses any
theory that ascribes our predicament to external
causes. "That which is wrong, first, foremost and most
undeniably, is Man."

Jung is only reiterating the Biblical analysis which pierces down below the surface and lays bare the inner nerve of man's malaise. There is something demonic in human nature, which turns our purest dreams to sorry disillusionment and our most strenuous endeavours to failure. But the Bible, in its penetrating analysis, goes further. It claims that evil is not merely a suggestive phenomenon, embedded in man's nature—it has also an objective existence, endemic in the very constitution of the universe. "We wrestle," said Paul, "not against flesh and blood, but against principalities, against powers, against the rulers of the darkness of this world, against spiritual wickedness in high places." The Bible, in taking sin seriously, offers us a profound analysis of the human predicament.

But it does more. It gives us *an answer to the human predicament*. It is one thing to analyse—it is another to offer a positive remedy. It is one thing to draw attention to our desperate plight, it is another to lead us out of the labyrinth of our hopelessness. There are any number of realistic books which scorn our shoddy sentimentalists and confront us with unpleasant facts, but they leave us bereft of all hope. This is true of *The Fall* by Albert Camus—a searing exposure of human altruism as a device which hides our inherent, incurable selfishness. And George Orwell's *1984* is also grim and realistic, but it leaves man at the end of the day disillusioned, damned and deprived of any future.

The Bible, on the other hand, though it stresses the demonic nature of evil in all its dimensions, pulsates from beginning to end with an unconquerable hope.

It holds the answer to our desperate human predicament: Jesus Christ, crucified, risen and triumphant. And it goes on to declare that it is only the death-defeating Christ who can cope effectively with all the fierce intractible enigmas of life. The Bible offers us no economic blue-print, no political utopia, no facile formula for social betterment, but it does offer us all the more abundant, the more exuberant, the more liberating life in Jesus Christ.

Whatever translation we use, Authorised Version or the very latest, this Book speaks to our condition. We are addressed by God out of its pages and confronted in our need by the living Christ. This was the experience of Augustine—the brilliant scholar with his glittering outward success and his constant inner defeat. In the orchard in Milan, he heard a voice say, "Take up and read". He opened his Bible and he read, "Put ye on the Lord Jesus Christ, and make not provision for the flesh." And immediately his chains fell off and he knew the meaning of release. It happened many centuries ago to Bishop Fisher of Rochester when they led him out of the Tower of London to his martyrdom. The sight of the scaffold unnerved him momentarily. Then he took his Latin New Testament out of his pocket, and, opening it at the 17th Chapter of the Gospel according to St. John, read, "This is life eternal, that they might know thee, the only true God, and Jesus Christ, whom thou has sent." Suddenly fear vanished and John Fisher said, "Blessed be God—this word will suffice for all eternity."

The Bible is not a peculiar ornament, a sword of

Goliath, once mighty in battle but now wrapped up in the cloth of veneration, and relegated to a fringe of existence where it lies inert and useless. Without the Bible we have no sword in our hand when we engage in the task of evangelism, to which every Church member stands committed. No doubt there are other instruments of Christian mission, but this is the supreme weapon, and, like David gazing at that peerless blade half-hidden behind the ephod, we too must cry out, "Give it to me, there is none like it."

This sermon was preached to the Presbytery of Stirling and Dunblane on the occasion of the publication of The New English Bible. It was an overture from this Presbytery that initiated the new translation.

5

THE MEANING OF THE SACRAMENT

"After the same manner also he took the cup, when he had supped, saying, This cup is the new testament in my blood: this do ye, as oft as ye drink it, in remembrance of me."

I Corinthians 11, 25

"THIS do in remembrance of me." These surely are the most familiar words in the Bible. They form part of the formula we repeat every time we celebrate the Lord's supper. They were in use even before Paul wrote his letter to the Christian Church at Corinth, and no doubt they will continue to be used by future generations as they sit down to keep this feast which stands at the very centre of the Church's life.

"This do in remembrance of me." This supper enacted by Christ in the Upper Room, is not a magical rite appealing to some superstitious sub-stratum of our nature. It is, in the words of Professor Emil Brunner, "an Illustrated Word of God". In it we are addressed, not through the ear as in preaching, but through the eye; not through speech but through action. Jesus knew what He was doing when He instituted this sacrament. Most people prefer the concrete to the abstract, so the greatest of all teachers taught us the truth about the character of God, through a simple meal.

The words of the institution point to the sacrament

as *a commemorative act*. The Lord's Supper reminds us that Christianity is rooted and grounded in history. The ancient Greeks had a pantheon of gods, Zeus, Venus and others, who dwelt in splendid isolation on the top of Mount Olympus—mythical creatures, products of poetic imagination. They had no historical reality. Very different is the Christ whom the first apostles hailed as Messiah and Lord, who had suffered under Pontius Pilate and was crucified when Tiberius Caesar reigned as Emperor, who belongs to the solid, tangible stuff of history. In Jesus of Nazareth we are dealing not with fancies, but with facts, every bit as hard and sharp as the nails that were hammered into His Cross.

In our own national history, certain events stand out. The defeat of the Spanish Armada, Waterloo and Trafalgar, the Battle of Britain. We remember them because they recall a danger that was overwhelming and a deliverance that bordered on the miraculous. But these victories, momentous as they are, pale into insignificance before the death of Jesus which we commemorate at Communion. This fact has embedded itself into our racial memory and has become irrevocably mixed up with our tradition. Empires have waxed and waned, fashionable philosophies have won and lost their appeal, cultures have come and gone, but this sacred meal endureth for ever.

And in celebrating the Sacrament, we are doing far more than remembering a great historical event, shrouded in the mists of antiquity: we are actually saluting a living person. "Do this in remembrance of me," said Jesus, thereby lifting his religion out of vague generalities and grounding it for ever in a personality. It is inconceivable that men and women should meet to remember Julius Caesar, Frederick the Great, or Napoleon Bonaparte, but it seems right and proper for us to assemble to pay homage to Jesus Christ. We are met to commemorate in the Sacrament not a dead fact, but a living person.

Again the words of the institution point to the sacrament as *a corporate act*. In sophisticated circles, even among good church people, there is a fashion to exalt the more elaborate ritual of the Roman Mass and the Anglican Holy Communion, at the expense of our own more austere rite. The reason for this vogue is no doubt a complex one and there is no point in discussing it here. But its sponsors seem to forget one thing, and it is this. The Reformed tradition shows forth the corporate spirit of communion better than any other—Roman, Anglican or Greek Orthodox. A Presbyterian does not go up as an individual to the Communion rail and receive the elements from an individual priest. He receives the bread and wine from his neighbour and passes them to his neighbour as they sit together round the Lord's Table. If symbolism is important, then it follows that the Reformed Communion demonstrates, not the individual, but the corporate aspect of the Christian faith, and the implications of this truth, if we understood them and acted on them, would revolutionise the whole of our society.

Experts who have studied this matter claim that

there is a resurgence of interest in the sacraments, not merely in Scotland, but throughout the whole world. Indeed, one of them assures me that the new vitality one senses in the Church of England stems from the recent practice of celebrating Communion at the family 11 o'clock service. This new feature we should welcome and applaud, but the acid test is whether the revived interest in Communion breaks down our social inhibitions and antagonisms and brings into being the Community of the Holy Spirit. If it fails in this, what we are seeing is a recrudescence of sacramentalism whose only effect will be that of blunting our spiritual sensitivities and sanctifying our traditional divisions.

In his book, *The Status Seekers*, Vance Packard describes some features of an affluent American society and draws our attention to one in particular—the creation of standardised one-community suburbs which are either all white, or all "white collar", all middle-class or all working-class, all Gentile or all Jewish. This tendency is not merely American, it is universal. We meet it in Africa, in Asia, in Britain and even in Soviet Russia, despite its claims to have created a classless society. Packard then goes on to defend some of these traditional European social divisions, exported to the new world, on the ground that they reduce psychological anxiety by making people more contented with their lot in life and their given status.

I don't know whether this is bad sociology, but it is certainly bad Christianity, and it is diametrically opposed to the message of the Lord's Supper which by emphasising the corporate aspect of our faith, thereby condemns our class-consciousness and our distorted sense of community. If we took the sacrament seriously and paid heed to its revolutionary message, we would examine, in the name of the Lord, every structure, including education, which not only bolsters but even encourages our social stratification. The Sacrament, if only we knew it, is a high, explosive shell, packed with dangerous dynamite. Work out its implications in society and we would discover that a great many of our traditional mental attitudes will be blown sky-high.

Once again the words of the institution point to the sacrament as *a sacrificial act*. The fundamental difference between the Roman Catholic and Protestant attitudes centres round the Mass. For the Romans, the Mass is a sacrifice the officiating priest offers up to God, and a work of merit credited to men and counted to them for righteousness. The Reformers turned a stern face to this conception and repudiated it utterly and decisively: they maintained that the sacrifice Jesus offered up on Calvary was perfect. There is no way in which a Church could add to or subtract from it. The Reformers took their stand on the finished work of Christ and we, who are the spiritual heirs, must on no account betray them.

Nevertheless, there is a sense in which we cannot get away from the idea of sacrifice, when we celebrate the sacrament. In his *Theology of the Sacraments*, Donald Baillie points out that the Greek verb '$\Pi o\iota\hat{\epsilon}\iota\nu$', translated "do" in most versions, has a wider meaning. It can mean "offer up", or "make a sacrifice". So the words of our text could read, "Offer up this in remembrance of me". There is perhaps a sense, therefore, in which Christians standing in the Reformed tradition, can be said to offer something to God in the sacrament.

In the sacrament, we can offer up our worship to God, and therein lies the need for discipline in Church attendance. If we have been slack and spasmodic in our worship, we cannot conscientiously offer it, for that would be an insult not only to our own intelligence and integrity, but also to God. Communion is the climax of Christian worship and this is one unerring test we can apply to it. Can we honestly offer it to God, laying it, as it were, on the altar of the Lord's broken body, or must we hang our heads in shame and say, "Woe is me for I have been grossly careless, and I can't offer to the Lord that which has not cost me anything."

Again, in the sacrament, we can offer up our work to God. On all hands we hear it said that our countrymen are not working as hard or as well as they might, and consequently production is falling and we are losing our export market to others. I don't know whether this is true or not, but if it is, what a heaven-sent opportunity for Christians! We must demonstrate to a cynical world that work is not a money-making concern but a sacramental vocation in which we give of our very best. We who partake of the elements symbolising the Lord's finished work must labour not primarily to promote our own interests or to impress others, but to please the God who in His wisdom ordained it.

Finally, in the sacrament, we offer up ourselves to God. In the Church of Scotland *Book of Common Order* and in the Church of England *Book of Common Prayer*, we say in the prayer of thanksgiving and consecration, "And here we offer and present to Thee ourselves, our souls and our bodies, to be a reasonable, holy and living sacrifice." We cannot give of our best till we give ourselves. A friend once visited Gauguin's studio and stood in front of each canvas surveying it critically. Before one of them he stood for a long time, arrested by something, an elusive but unmistakable quality none of the others seemed to possess. And as he groped after the indefinable something, Gauguin spoke up, "Yes, you are right. That is my best. It is the only one in which I have put the whole of myself." It is not possible to produce great art, great religion or great living, till we are prepared to offer ourselves totally, keeping nothing in reserve. Then and only then can God use us to further His mighty purpose for mankind.

SECTION IV

MISCELLANEOUS

K

INTRODUCTION

The preacher may find himself in the position of a certain professor of Zoology who, on discovering a type of seaweed that fitted his definition neither of a plant nor an animal, felt it had no right to exist. Our reason classifies but does not create, so we must not make the mistake of squeezing the living message out of sermons by classifying them too neatly.

A living sermon is no more to be dissected than a living person. It may be legitimate to describe a sermon as doctrinal or apologetic or expository, according to the dominant emphasis, but it is not possible to draw any sharp divisions. A good sermon, in order to speak to as many people as possible, must be a blend of all these elements. Our subject matter is God's revelation of Himself, therefore it follows that preaching plays havoc with all our neat, nicely defined homiletical systems.

I hope that the five sermons in this section illustrate what I am trying to express. In preparing and delivering them, I have not been conscious of having stressed any one dominant note. I trust, however, that in each case I have used the text to show how piercingly relevant the Christian faith is to the problems of man and society.

THE NEED FOR MALADJUSTMENT

"And be not conformed to this world, but ye be
transformed by the renewing of your mind that ye
may prove what is that good, and acceptable, and
perfect will of God."

Romans 12, 2

IT was in the sixteenth century that the ideal of the
gentleman emerged, and the gentleman was a person
in whom manners were more important than morals,
in whom self-control was the supreme virtue, in whom
manliness had become incarnate. This image has
exercised a considerable influence over our culture,
but of late it has been pushed into the background.

Another image has emerged—that of the well-
adjusted person. Modern life has become so maddeningly complex that the incidence of nervous break-down
is on the increase. Therefore it is not at all surprising
that our ambition is to turn out, not the classical,
stereotyped gentleman, but the poised, self-assured,
well-adjusted individual.

This is the aim of the psychologist who is faced with
a very difficult problem indeed. His job is to take a
person, torn apart by emotional conflict, and after
treatment to restore him to society in one piece. For
the remainder of his life such a person may be doomed
to walk the tight-rope of adjustment, but he has the

satisfaction of knowing he is at least a useful citizen.

This is the aim of big business. In his book, *The Lonely Crowd*, David Riesman claims that business organisations impose an ethic of conformity, and in his, *Affluent Society*, Professor A. J. Galbraith argues that the masses are treated as tools. Under the bombardment of advertising slogans and suggestions, their wants become synonymous with those of their neighbours. They are made to adjust themselves to an economy whose main object is to induce them to buy things whether they need them or not.

This is precisely the danger lurking in the modern media of communication—in the newspaper, wireless and television, even in a free society. They may succeed in hammering the malleable masses into an attitude of mind which will accept without question the prejudices of the majority. Thus when the abolition of capital punishment was before Parliament a few years ago, the largest daily in this country argued, "The majority of people want capital punishment, therefore its retention is morally right." I have heard the same argument applied to Premium Bonds. It never seems to occur to such people that there was a time when the overwhelming majority believed the earth was flat, that kings had divine right, that the moon caused lunacy; yet they happened to be wrong. But we should not feel superior, for in more ways than we care to confess, we have all come to terms with the pressures of a conformist society.

To be sure, a certain measure of adjustment is necessary, and it is no use pretending otherwise. But at the same time, there are values and presuppositions accepted by the many, which Christians must be prepared to question. The words of our text were written to Christians in Rome living under the dictatorship of Caesar, and the temptation to conform must have been well-nigh irresistible. Yet this is what the Apostle says, "Be not conformed to this world, but be ye transformed by the renewing of your mind, that ye may prove what is that good, and acceptable, and perfect will of God." What then are the logical implications of this Apostolic injunction?

One inescapable implication is that Christians must be prepared to be maladjusted to their society—"Be not conformed to this world." There are experts who argue that in the interests of mental health and emotional stability, it is better to come to terms with the accepted standards of the community. If this is so, it follows inexorably that we can attach little blame to a man like Eichmann. It could be said that submission to Hitler enabled the individual to adjust himself to an unpleasant situation with the minimum amount of discomfort. But the fact remains that there were people in Germany who did not conform. They chose maladjustment and suffered accordingly.

We cannot witness effectively in a corrupt society till we are prepared not only to question the sanctity of the *status quo*, but if necessary, to defy it. History bristles with examples—Jeremiah in the Old Testament, Luther in the sixteenth century, Wilberforce and Shaftesbury in the nineteenth. Most of all, it was true of Jesus. If he had placed the accent on conformity, and accepted the unexamined presuppositions of His society, He would have aroused no antagonism. Jesus refused to come to terms. The Cross on which He died was the full measure of His maladjustment.

There are a number of deeply ingrained attitudes in our society today to which people tend to conform, and on all Christians facing them, there is laid the sacred duty of maladjustment. One is the attitude to war. The feverish building of atomic shelters in America, encouraged by big business, implies its inevitability, if not indeed its imminence. When will we see that war in an atomic age is far more ridiculous and infinitely more immoral than the human sacrifices the ancients once offered to mythical divinities?

Another attitude, sanctified by tradition, is the one towards race. Only a sentimentalist will speak in terms of an easy solution. But Christians must become maladjusted to the myth of white supremacy. There is no justification, Christian or otherwise, for the racial segregation that condemns one complexion of skin to perpetual servitude, and glorifies the other as the permanent boss. It is not possible to be Christian in any significant sense till we are maladjusted to a sinful society.

There is another inescapable implication stemming from Paul's injunction, and it is this. Christians must be prepared to use their minds, "Be ye transformed by the renewing of your mind."

We are apt to think of Paul's conversion exclusively in terms of a mystical experience in which he saw through the veil of the temporal, right to the heart of the Eternal. And there is a profound sense in which this is true, but it is by no means the whole truth. On the Damascus road Paul experienced a Copernican revolution, not only in his soul but also in his mind, and he spent three years in solitude working out the far-reaching repercussions of this momentous event. Paul attached little importance to a conversion that amounted only to a stirring of the emotions. He knew that a man is not really changed till his intellect is captured, till he is transformed by the renewing of his mind.

During the first few centuries, Christianity, though a minority sect, made a tremendous impact upon a pagan world. No doubt there are various reasons for its success, but one is the fact that on all the big issues Christians out-thought their contemporaries. This does not mean that the new religion was a high-brow philosophy catering only for the cultured *élite*. It was, as a matter of fact, addressed to ordinary people, but it stabbed their slumbering minds awake and made men of them intellectually.

At the time I came to this congregation, an older minister gave me a piece of gratuitous advice. "Remember! No theology in the pulpit! I used to preach theology till one of my devoutest members—a Professor of Science—took me aside and gave me the best advice I have ever had. 'During the week,' the man of learning argued, 'I deal with intellectual problems, and on Sunday I come to Church looking for a message of comfort and cheer'." My friend dutifully obliged. It never seemed to occur to him that in his own subject the Professor in question was an original, brilliant, provocative thinker, but that in his religion he was intellectually at the Sunday School level.

This, I am afraid, is true of most educated people in Britain today. They support the Church, participate in its worship, contribute to its causes, but they seldom, if ever, read a serious book on religion. Meantime the yeast of intellectual revolution is seething and bubbling and fermenting in the world outside. The prospects for the Church are exceedingly dim, till it relates its message intelligently to the desperate problems of a perplexed age. Christians will effect no radical change, in themselves or others, till they are transformed by the renewing of their minds.

There is one more implication that follows from the text—Christian obedience is totalitarian, "That ye may prove what is that good and acceptable and perfect will of God."

The New Testament does not draw any clear-cut distinction between the message of Christ on the one hand, and the response of man on the other. The Church, even in its worst hours, has demanded some sort of obedience from its members. This is undoubtedly so; but, at the same time, it has been consistently guilty of distorting the meaning of Christian obedience and narrowing the sphere of its operation in society.

The fallacy we have to explode is the one which assumes that religion is a private affair, a perpendicular relationship between man and his God, which is nobody else's business—as Lord Melbourne, the Victorian, used to assert with great truculence. Lord Melbourne's politics are relegated to the melancholy archives of a forgotten past, but his religious principles still flourish.

Not for a moment would I deny the truth in the assertion that religion is a private affair. How could I, when Jesus Himself said that the inner meaning of faith is experienced in solitude, in a room with the door shut? But Jesus did not leave it there. He also went on to say, "The Kingdom of Heaven is likened unto leaven which a woman took and hid in three measures of meal, till the whole was leavened." So Jesus was thinking not merely of the leaven—the hidden vital relationship between the seeking soul and the answering God, but also of the whole lump—the entire world, its politics, its intricate social relationships, its industry and education, till it was all leavened.

What do we mean by Christian obedience? It is illustrated by an incident which took place in New Orleans, a city always simmering, and at times boiling over, with racial tension, A certain Mr. and Mrs. Gabrielle incurred the hostility of the community by sending their children to a desegregated school in obedience to the supreme court's injunction. Their only supporters were a Methodist minister and a Roman Catholic priest, yet they stood firm against every form of vilification and persecution. Their toughest opponents were devout Church-goers who lined the road, brandishing their Bibles and hissing, "Nigger-lovers", as the Gabrielles escorted their children into school.

This courageous couple have demonstrated the meaning of Christian obedience not only to their own race-conscious community, but to the whole world.

They have shown dramatically that religion, far from being a private luxury, makes totalitarian demands. No doubt, the roots of the faith that sustains them go deep. They lie deep in the hidden secret relationship between the solitary soul and the all-inclusive God—but the branches reach out far and wide, intertwining themselves with such questions as race, prejudice, education, and what to do when the most influential people in the community organise themselves against us. The word, obedience, belongs to a distinctively Christian vocabulary. We must continue to use it, only we must give it a wider and more revolutionary meaning.

2

GOD IN EXILE

"By the rivers of Babylon, there we sat down, yea, we wept, when we remembered Zion.

We hanged our harps upon the willows in the midst thereof.

For there they that carried us away captive required of us a song; and they that wasted us required of us mirth, saying, Sing us one of the songs of Zion.

How shall we sing the Lord's song in a strange land?"

Psalm 137, 1–4

To understand this plaintive cry we must hear it against a grim, historical background. The author was an exile, deported during one of the wars that so frequently devastated ancient Israel. Displaced persons, without the faintest hope of repatriation, they enshrined their hopelessness in words that still haunt us—"By the rivers of Babylon, there we sat down, yea, we wept when we remembered Zion."

A despised minority, subjected to massive pressures and bombarded by hostile propaganda, these exiled Hebrews found it extremely hard to preserve their national identity. Jehovah, supreme in Israel, was not even recognised in Babylon, where the pantheon of Marduk', Bel and Mergal held sway. In such an uncongenial environment it became more difficult than ever to keep the first commandment—"Thou shalt have no other gods before me."

Furthermore, their jealously guarded and carefully preserved way of life infuriated their overlords. That they had become butts of cruel ridicule, and targets of savage derision is clear from the words, "For they that carried us away captive required of us a song; and they that wasted us required of us mirth, saying, Sing us one of the songs of Zion. How can we sing the Lord's song in a strange land?"

Never has the problem of a suffocating secularism been more felicitously expressed. What really disturbed those Hebrew exiles was the desolating thought that the God who was so active and articulate in Israel, was hopelessly impotent in an alien land. This is still our basic fear. How many of us feel that the God who was so much to the fore in the age of Cromwell and the Covenanters, and even much later when Gladstone quoted Scripture in the House of Commons, is now strangely quiescent and inert? Sartre and Camus, in their novels, philosophies and plays, articulate the unspoken suspicion of many when they claim that "God is dead".

Even when the sun of Victorian optimism was still shining in all its noonday brightness, there were pessimists like Matthew Arnold, who felt that the retreat of Christianity had already begun, and that in time the Church would be no more than a deserted island in the middle of an encircling ocean of vast indifference.

The Sea of Faith
Was once, too, at the full and round earth's shore
Lay like the folds of a bright girdle furled.
But now I only hear its melancholy, long, withdrawing roar,
Retreating, to the breath
Of the night-wind, down the vast edges drear
And naked shingles of the world.

The difficulties confronting Christians today are truly gigantic, but when were circumstances ever favourable for religion, we may ask? Certainly not when the Hebrews hung their harps upon the willows by the alien waters of Babylon. Certainly not when Paul experienced the full blast of Nero's demonic fury and was executed in Rome. Certainly not when Luther nailed his *95 Articles* to the door of the castle church and by this signal act of courage brought a new world into being. Certainly not when John Knox and his fellow-Reformers raised their voices in a Scotland which was, perhaps, at that time the most backward and barbarous country in Europe.

Still the agonising question remains—how can we communicate the Christian faith convincingly in a society where the attitude to the Church ranges from a venomous hostility to a well-bred sophisticated indifference? How can we Christianise the disgruntled industrial masses that regard the Church as the bastion of an iniquitous *status quo*? How can we win back the lost respect of intellectuals, who assume God is a displaced person, both in the universe and in the individual's experience, and who are impervious to the traditional methods of evangelism? How can we preach the gospel in a world where change outpaces our powers of adaptation? Essentially our problem is the same as that of the Hebrew exiles by the rivers of Babylon, "How can we sing the Lord's song in a strange land?" Well then, how did they preserve their identity and at the same time extend the range of their influence in a pagan environment?

One way of singing the Lord's song in a strange land is by *personal commitment*. These exiles found themselves face to face with an either/or decision. On the one hand, they could succumb to inescapable pressures, come to terms with shoddy values, and in the process lose their faith. Or, on the other hand, they could elect to be true to their spiritual heritage and stand firm whatever the cost. Their steadfastness when subjected to cruel testing is indicated by the moving words, "If I forget thee, O Jerusalem, let my right hand forget her cunning. If I do not remember thee, let my tongue cleave to the roof of my mouth."

We are prepared to concede this. Personal commitment is highly desirable. Psychologically it has a beneficial effect on personality, but is such a thing really possible in a bewildering world where all the traditional landmarks seem to have been obliterated? It is all very well asking people to decide, but to whom or to what are they supposed to give their unswerving allegiance? To this question various answers have been given.

There is the answer of Omar Khayyam. An Epicurean in conduct, he nevertheless sought guidance by amassing the opinions of others and pondering the distilled wisdom of the ages. And this is his depressing verdict:

Myself when young did eagerly frequent
Doctor and Saint; and heard great Argument
About it and about, but ever more
Came out by the same door as in I went.

There is the answer of Hamlet. Hyper-sensitive to
the stresses and challenges of a maddeningly complex
life, he was never able to come to a clear-cut decision.
He found himself, as indeed so many of us do, perpetually balancing pros and cons, for ever oscillating from
one mood to another to the tune of "to be or not to be".

And there is the answer of Christ. No one can honestly
accuse him of oversimplifying the complexities of life.
He saw the Cross a long way off looming over the
horizon, and in the sternest terms He warned His
followers that persecution was the inevitable consequence of Christian discipleship. This is so, but at
the same time He insisted that if a man was to arrive at
ultimate truth, and lay hold of the living God, he had
to take sides. Here he left no possible room for doubt.
His words are clear and sharp and unequivocal, "Not
every one that saith unto me, Lord, Lord, shall enter
into the Kingdom of Heaven, but he that doeth the
will of my Father which is in Heaven."

Another way of singing the Lord's song in a strange
land is by *corporate worship*. For the Christian it goes
without saying that there is no adequate substitute for
personal commitment, but by itself this is not enough.
No man, however tenacious, can withstand in isolation
a prolonged assault on his soul. That is why both the
Nazis and the Communists put a man in solitary con-
finement, before they proceeded to break him down

L

and brain-wash him. The psalmist significantly used not the singular but the plural sense when he asked, "How can we sing the Lord's song in a strange land?"

Someone may object with a just cynicism that worship makes no iota of difference to people. It does not in any radical sense broaden their sympathies, dispel their prejudices, or sharpen their vision of the world's need. It may even confirm them in error by sanctifying their unexamined attitudes and strengthening their mistaken allegiances.

This I am afraid is too tragically true, but to be fair we must judge the importance of worship, not by its worst but by its best effects. "To worship," writes the late William Temple, "is to quicken the conscience by the holiness of God, to feed the mind by the truth of God, to purge the imagination by the beauty of God, to open the heart to the love of God." And according to the philosopher, Professor John Macmurray, worship exerts a democratising and a stabilising influence upon the community.

Worship, properly understood and actively engaged in, helps in two directions. For one thing it does away with our proud self-centred solitariness. This is so, because in every act of worship we associate ourselves not only with our neighbours in the pew, but also with the countless multitudes of believers who reach back to Christ Himself in the Upper Room. We are part of the universal fellowship that stretches across the earth, and back through the ages, and up into the unseen world. In worship we sing the song of our common humanity: "Therefore with angels and archangels and

all the company of heaven, we adore and magnify Thy
Holy Name."

And for another thing, worship helps us in the hour
of temptation and critical emergency. It enables us "to
stand in the evil day, and having done all, to stand."
It intensifies our fragile perceptions and fortifies our
fluctuating aspirations. When we were children we all
played the game of holding a magnifying-glass over a
piece of paper, till the rays of the sun, concentrated on
a single spot, burned a hole through it. We know, of
course, that the magnifying-glass did not increase the
sun's power, only focussed it, thereby making it more
effective at a particular point. So in worship—"My
soul doth magnify the Lord." In this corporate act we
make God great in our lives and are immeasurably
strengthened thereby.

We can sing the Lord's song in a strange land by
personal commitment and corporate worship, but these
by no means exhaust all the possibilities—we can also
do it by *intelligent witness*. In Glasgow I once saw a
sad spectacle in one of the main streets, crowded with
shoppers on a busy Saturday afternoon. A man with a
desperately doleful expression on his face, kept walking
up and down carrying a large sandwich-board on his
back, on which were inscribed the words—"How can
ye escape the damnation of hell—repent and be saved."
He did this for hours with the utmost sincerity, never
once thinking that, far from attracting, he was most
definitely alienating those to whom the message was
directed. This is the wrong way to witness.

I know a religious sect in this country whose members

refuse to eat or drink with any outside their own group. They base their conduct on such verses in Scripture as, "Come out from among them and be ye separate," or, "What fellowship has righteousness with unrighteousness?" And they blandly ignore the somewhat disconcerting fact that Jesus ate with publicans and sinners, consorted with the riff-raff of society, kept company with unsavoury characters like Mary Magdalen, Matthew and Zaccheus. This is the wrong kind of witness.

The overwhelming majority of Church members are by no means as narrow. On the contrary, they are broadminded, cultured, urbane, and for them there is no crude and obvious dichotomy between God and the world. Only on one point they are adamant—religion must on no account be mixed up with political and social questions. That is anathema. They tell you they come to church to be comforted, not to be disturbed, and that all those complex questions should be left to the professional politicians or to the qualified economists. When you point out to them that the policy they are advocating was precisely the one followed by Stalin and by Hitler, they don't turn a hair. This is the wrong kind of witness.

If our witness is to be intelligent and effective, it must be total. It must address itself to men's minds and bodies as well as to their souls. It must speak not only to the individual in his solitariness, but also to society in the whole arena of its convulsive agonies and pressing needs. Let us not delude ourselves into thinking that Christian witness is easy in an acquisitive, affluent society, and we must not look for ready-made techniques, glib answers, or smooth formulae. The sole thing we can be reasonably certain of is that we can only witness for Christ in the measure in which we are prepared to get mixed up with the world for which He died. We must become inextricably involved in the dilemmas of society, its political crises, its social challenges, its systems of economics and education, before we can in any meaningful sense sing the Lord's song in a strange land.

3

MONSTER IN THE DEEP

"Canst thou draw out leviathan with an hook?"

Job 41, 1

"CANST thou draw out leviathan with an hook?" Job is, of course, referring to the crocodile, and this chapter in which he portrays him is one of the most descriptive passages in literature. The language is strong and sinewy and poetic. As we read it we can conjure up an image of this cruel and sinister animal in all its terrifying malevolence. We can see the track of its hard spiky body in the mud, the spray spouting from its nostrils as it submerges, the water lashed into boiling foam when it is angry. We can almost hear the savage snap of its gigantic jaws. So with delicious irony Job poses the question: Is anyone naïve enough to suppose that he can go fishing for the crocodile with an ordinary line and hook?

The ancients were so impressed by the ferocity of the crocodile that leviathan, the name they gave it, in time became a symbol of monstrous tyranny whatever shape it happened to assume. In the Old Testament leviathan stood for the powerful enemies of Israel—Egypt, Assyria, Babylon; while in the New Testament it was another name for the cult of Caesar, the brutal dictatorship which threatened to trample the struggling infant Church out of existence.

And what does leviathan symbolise for us today? Surely this—the principle of evil embedded in history without and in human nature within. Just as the crocodile, sprawling in the slimy mud, was an object of terror for primitive people, so evil confronts us everywhere in modern society, savage and sinister and indestructible. It is a hydra-headed monster, which when suppressed at one point obtrudes itself at another. Sometimes it assumes the form of a demonic dictatorship, holding the individual in contempt; sometimes that of a corrupt and acquisitive democracy, lacking all sense of direction. We see it also in the shape of mass violence, crime and juvenile delinquency. There are even occasions when it exudes an odour of sanctity conjoined with worldliness within the Church itself.

And what does the hook symbolise? Man's incredible naïveté where evil is concerned, his chattering complacency in face of this monstrous and universal fact, the ludicrous ineffectiveness of all his efforts to dislodge it from his world, his impotence in the grip of this deadly malaise. "Canst thou draw out leviathan with an hook?" Yes, Job's sarcasm speaks to our condition. Evil is a terrifying reality. It is not possible to evade it or to argue it out of existence. And this is the question. Are we able to control it by the hooks of our own human contrivance?

First, let us consider the hook we call scientific knowledge. Never has it been wielded with greater skill and dexterity than it is at the present moment, and beyond any argument it has succeeded in taming some of man's most vicious enemies. Epidemics that once swept continents, decimating entire populations, have been controlled and rendered impotent by it. It has wrested its closely guarded secrets from Nature and harnessed them to human use. Not only has it mastered the air and annihilated distance, but it is now in process of conquering space itself. Perhaps it is not so very surprising that men have come to look upon it as the one and only saviour.

But today we are not at all as cock-a-hoop and confident as we used to be. We have seen the hook of scientific mastery used not merely against disease and ignorance and poverty, but against personality itself. Isn't this the sinister thing about what goes by the name of brain washing? And wasn't this precisely the most frightening aspect of Nazism? It took root and sprouted in a country noted for the mastery of scientific technique. And it used this knowledge to pervert human values and to put back the clock of civilisation.

Hence the new spirit of humility, sometimes amounting to guilt, evident among the leading scientists. The reason why so many of them are so passionately opposed to nuclear weapons is that they now see the No. 1 enemy of civilisation as not the hydrogen bomb, but human nature itself. Professor J. R. Oppenheimer, the American atomic physicist who was largely responsible for producing the first bomb, of late confessed that he has never been able to shake off his sense of guilt. In constructing the bomb in the first place, and dropping it on defenceless people in the second, scientists had succumbed to evil, and no amount of glib rationalisations can efface this searing fact.

Human nature, not the megaton bomb, is the leviathan that threatens our existence on this planet today.

Second, let us consider the hook we call social reform. Whatever our final estimate, we must on no account belittle its magnificent achievements. Social legislation in Britain, as in America and Russia, has many notable victories to its credit. It has practically eliminated poverty from all civilised countries, and in our welfare states it cares for, some would say coddles, people from the cradle to the grave. Communism is based on the belief that evil is a purely social phenomenon, and that intelligent legislation can not only curb it but usher in the perfected order of our dreams. But can such a claim stand up to scrutiny?

Sir Sydney Smith, in a lecture he gave to a teachers' conference some years ago, drew their attention to a challenging fact. He pointed out that over the last fifty years there has been a progressive improvement in social conditions. The working man enjoys higher wages, better educational facilities and a greater measure of security than ever before. The masses have wider opportunities for sport and every form of recreation. The treatment of criminals is more humane. In short, if social reform were the determining factor, we should expect a diminishing crime sheet in this country. What then is the position? It is this. Serious crime, like rape, robbery with violence, and murder, has leapt from 3 per thousand in 1900 to 11 per thousand in 1952. Sir Sydney ended his lecture with the words, "Crime has not been favourably affected by attempts at reform and rehabilitation." The same thought could be expressed more picturesquely and more pointedly in the words of Job, "Canst thou draw out leviathan with an hook?"

Third, let us consider the hook we call psychological adjustment. The psychologists are in process of becoming the priestly caste of modern society. Their prestige has grown in direct ratio to the steep rise in nervous disorder. There are various types of mental illness which the ordinary doctor and the ordinary minister can't cope with, and so men and women in increasing numbers turn to the psychiatrist, because they feel he alone is able to hold out a ray of hope.

Those of us who have some experience in dealing with the emotionally disturbed and the mentally distraught are grateful for what psychiatry is trying to do. But at the same time we feel it is sentimental naïveté to imagine that psychological adjustment is the answer to all the ills the human flesh is heir to; or that it can eradicate self-centredness which is of the very essence of sin. This is how Professor Jung, the most celebrated of all modern psychiatrists, sums up the problem— "No Gordian knot can be cut by psychotherapy, for it has the awkward property of always tying itself again."

This is so because the psychiatrist is himself a prey to self-centredness. He, too, is tainted with the curse of Adam. In theory he may have a prescription for anxiety, but in practice he is in bondage like the rest of us and needs deliverance. The novel, *Mine own Executioner*, takes this human contradiction as its main theme. The hero is a psychologist who though he can diagnose and cure the ills of others, is himself a victim of libidinous impulses and anti-social attitudes in whose grip he is powerless. But why should this surprise us? The leviathan of evil lurking in the subterranean depth of human nature can't be drawn out by the bent pin of psycho-analysis.

A precondition of salvation is the taking of evil seriously, and this is precisely what our lesser literature today studiously avoids. It weaves its plots round the trivial, the ephemeral, the inconsequential, and contrives either an impossibly happy, or a synthetically sordid ending. How very different with men like Job and Aeschylus and Shakespeare. Evil haunts them. They perpetually grapple with it, and though they offer no positive answer, they make it clear that it defies all the hooks of our human contrivance and ingenuity.

This, curiously enough, is the theme of Herman Melville's *Moby Dick*. The irony is that though it is a favourite with all boys it is at the same time one of the profoundest works in the English language. Ostensibly it is an adventure story. It tells how the ship, *Pequoad*, set off to hunt whales in the South Atlantic, and how the captain, called Ahab, became obsessed with a white whale—a killer nicknamed "Moby Dick". The destruction of Moby Dick became his one passion, and to this end he was prepared to sacrifice his ship, his crew and himself. With a kind of predetermined logic, the story ends by Moby Dick smashing the whaler to smithereens and killing those, including Captain Ahab, who dared question his malign supremacy.

Fundamentally this story is a parable—a parable of

the mystery of evil, and the malice inherent in the
universe. The white whale stands for the brute energies
of life, blind, senseless, overpowering, and Captain
Ahab stands for the spirit of man, pitting its puniness
against this savage might. And the evil is, of course
mixed up with the good. The mild whales which are
caught, cut up and turn to oil, stand for the things we
all hunt for—the domestic values and virtues—a happy
marriage, a good job, a modest modicum of success;
when suddenly, heaving its bulk out of the calm sea of
congenial circumstances, we see the other side of life—
the white whale of tragedy and human malevolence
and frustration. To fight them in our own strength is
hopeless. In their merciless grip we are as powerless as
Captain Ahab was when he pitted his courage against
the destructive fury and devilish malice of Moby
Dick.

If we can discern some kinship between the novel,
Moby Dick, and the New Testament, the contrast is
far more noticeable. Captain Ahab, it is true, did not
run away from evil, but in grappling with it, he was
destroyed. Jesus Christ did not turn His back to the
problem of evil either. He deliberately chose the way
of the Cross, and on the gaunt hill, outside the city wall,
He fought the concentrated malevolence of life and
conquered once and for all. It was because God knew
that our human palliatives for sin were useless, that all
our carefully contrived hooks, our wisdom, our knowledge, our courageous assaults, could not enable us to
meet leviathan on equal terms, that He sent Christ
into the world.

O loving wisdom of our God
When all was sin and shame,
A second Adam to the fight
And to the rescue came.

O wisest love! that flesh and blood
Which did in Adam fail
Should strive afresh against the foe,
Should strive and should prevail.

"Canst thou draw out leviathan with an hook?" This sarcasm pricks the bubble of our blasé complacency. It is time to stop deluding ourselves. The adversary we fight is strong and subtle and ruthless. And our deepest need is not a diagnosis of the mystery of evil, but deliverance from its malevolent power. A radical disease demands a radical remedy, and Jesus Christ, incarnate, crucified, risen, is the answer "Wherefore take unto you the whole armour of God, that ye may be able to withstand in the evil day, and having done all, to stand."

4

THE PARADOX OF
CHRISTIAN EXPERIENCE

" As sorrowful, yet always rejoicing."

II Corinthians 6, 10

THE poet, Swinburne, more perhaps by the hypnotic spell of his jingling verse than by the profundity of his thought, popularised the notion that the ancient pagan world was carefree and light-hearted and happy. Then came Christianity casting its dark and sombre shadows the way a cloud does when it comes between us and the sun. Jesus, far from liberating people and leading them into a fuller life, had actually infected them with a morbid sense of guilt. The only legacy he bequeathed to posterity was one of lasting gloom:

> Thou hast conquered, O pale Galilean,
> The world has grown grey from Thy breath.
> We have drunken of things Lethean
> And fed on the fullness of death.

Traditional religious art lends a certain amount of support to Swinburne's contention. The limp, pain-drenched figure of the crucifix does not strike us as the incarnation of joy. The Christ portrayed by the painters of the past is a life-denying ascetic, "a man of sorrows and acquainted with grief". The atmosphere of pathos that surrounds Him is enhanced by the never absent crown of thorns.

In the course of history there have appeared various expressions of Puritanism which in the main have been life-denying. The body was looked upon not as "the temple of the Holy Ghost", but as the repository of every kind of animal instinct and lascivious impulse. The robust and exuberant vitalities of our nature were damped down and held in iron check. The accent was put on inhibition rather than on emancipation. Francis Thompson apparently was a victim of this bleak and sterile philosophy. In his poem, "The Hound of Heaven", he describes in colourful detail his headlong flight from an austere and repellent Saviour. He rejected Christ because accepting Him meant a stunted, shrivelled up, impoverished existence.

> Yet was I sore adread
> Lest, having Him, I must have naught beside.

This caricature of New Testament Christianity could not last. The pendulum of revolt was bound to swing, and it has with a vengeance. Puritanism is now a term of opprobrium, a dirty word in our English vocabulary. There are Christians who dread this stigma so much that in order to avoid it, they are prepared to go to pathetic extremes. So, broadmindedness has come to be regarded as a cardinal virtue, and the pursuit of happiness as the *summum bonum* of our existence. The latter day apostles of sunshine and strenuous bonhomie are a numerous breed. From every pore of their being they exude the rollicking optimism of the American musical play *Oklahoma*. They go through the world not feeling the "burthen of the mystery", but shouting from the house-tops:

> I have a wonderful feeling
> Everything's going my way.

It does not even occur to them that this bogus cheer is as terrible a travesty of Christianity as the most dismal brand of medieval post-mortem other-worldliness.

Men have always assumed that the pursuit of happiness was not only a highly desirable end in itself, but that it was even divinely ordained. In that classical document, "The American Constitution", it is called an inalienable right—a privilege which cannot be surrendered or transferred to anyone else. The Bible makes no such claim. Contrary to our pleasure-seeking philosophies, it assumes that no man has a right to be deliriously happy as long as his neighbour is miserable.

It would be fatuous to describe the Christian either as an optimist or as a pessimist, for the simple reason that these words do not even begin to do justice to the paradoxical nature of his experience. Paul, with typical profundity, realises that no neat formula can express the sense of inescapable tension which is the legacy of every sincere believer. There is, indeed, a sense in which every healthy Christian must be a split personality. He goes through life "as sorrowful, yet always rejoicing".

The Christian is one who sorrows over the sufferings of humanity. In his novel, *La Peste*, Albert Camus describes a bubonic plague that broke out in the city

of Oran, decimating an entire population. Sympathetic-
ally he portrays a priest whose first reaction to the
tragedy was one of lofty self-righteousness. The people
of this town are a stiff-necked, adulterous, God-denying
generation, he argues, and this Divine retribution is
something they richly deserve. But as the plague spread
and the bodies of men, women and children were seen
stacked up, waiting for mass burial, his righteousness
evaporated and in its place he felt a vast pity and a
burning desire to help. From that moment he identified
himself with the victims, nursing them, comforting
them, tenderly administering the last rights, till in the
end he himself fell prey to the evil scourge.

Modern science may have succeeded in banishing our
plagues and pestilences, but it has not banished our
sorrows. Suffering is woven into the fabric of our
existence and is part of the meaning of life. Only in the
measure in which we are sensitive to it, and become
sacrificially involved in it, will the world take us
seriously. This is why Albert Schweitzer has touched
the imagination and evoked the admiration of our
age.

Again, the Christian is one who sorrows over the
injustices of life. How often have we heard it said that
backward people are happy the way they are, and that
we who enjoy the benefits of civilisation have no right
to disturb them. Well, they may be happy, though I
have always doubted this, but we who believe in the
Fatherhood of God have no right to be happy. Every
injustice that degrades man is an affront to God, and
those of us who profess Christ as Lord ought not to

M

rest till all such indignities are banished from the face of the earth.

No man can be a Christian without imaginative sympathy. That is why it is so blasphemous to discuss segregation as an abstraction permitting differences of opinion. The question every man must ask himself is, "How would I like to be treated as a second class citizen?" All the reforms, the revolutions and liberating movements of history have sprung out of this imaginative capacity for sitting where other people sit.

And the Christian must sorrow over his own sins. It has become fashionable to take men like Martin Luther, George Fox and John Bunyan, and in the light of modern psychological knowledge to explain how they acted in the way they did. Guilt-ridden introverts, they were apparently victims of what we now call anxiety-neurosis. We are left with the impression that if psycho-analysis had been practised in those far-off, pre-Freudian days, we would never have heard of the Society of Friends, Pilgrim's Progress, or, for that matter, the Reformation.

No doubt our fathers were more introspective than we are—at times morbidly so—but surely this is a shade healthier than the spectacle of professional writers placarding their moral perversions in public. We have reached a sorry impasse when it is now the accepted thing to be contemptuous of respectability and lyrical over depravity. When even Christian sophisticates resent any conduct that is not stained with sin and wobbly with ambiguity, it is time we lay awake at night and sweated a little over our condition.

Sorrow is an essential ingredient of the Christian life, but it must never be obtrusive. It must be counter-balanced by joy without which Christianity is like blood drained of its red corpuscles. We could even push this metaphor further and claim that sorrow and joy are the white and red corpuscles in the blood stream of the faith. Let there be any disproportion, and what is left is not red-blooded Christianity, but a sad and anaemic imitation of the real thing. In T. S. Eliot's play, *Murder in the Cathedral*, Thomas à Becket preaches his last sermon on Christmas day, 1170. He points out to the congregation that on the day after Christmas the Church significantly has always celebrated the death of its first martyr, Stephen. Is this an accident, he asks? By no means; "Just as we rejoice and mourn in the Birth and Passion of our Lord, so also in a smaller degree, we both rejoice and mourn in the death of martyrs." There, Thomas à Becket was only drawing our attention to the nature of Christian experience so succinctly expressed in Paul's paradox, "As sorrowful, yet always rejoicing".

Sorrow is ever with us. It is no more possible to flee from it than it is from our own shadow, but we must be careful not to exaggerate the place it has in the Christian life. Even in the midst of tragedy, we must on no account forget that there are solid grounds for rejoicing, and that in a world of blasted hopes, our joy no man can take from us.

The Christian rejoices in the knowledge that God exists. In his *Writer's Diary*, Somerset Maugham describes the sense of exhilaration he experienced when he became an atheist. A heavy burden rolled off his conscience and for the first time in his life he felt carefree and happy.

This is understandable, at least up to a point. Atheism offers a number of immediate advantages, but at best they are transitory and illusory. Sooner or later, despite a multitude of absorptions and distractions, there sets in a weariness of the spirit. This is the inevitable consequence of the God-shaped blank in the modern heart. No man can know the meaning of joy if he suspects that the universe is a fluke and that life signifies nothing. But the Christian exults in the belief that when the storm is at its fiercest, a strong hand rests upon the helm of things.

Again, the Christian rejoices in the knowledge that God cares. In ancient Rome, sensitive and cultured spirits had for generations protested in vain against the butcheries of the arena. The contests continued till one day a Christian monk, by the name of Telemachius, leapt into the arena and, thrusting himself between two gladiators, cried, "In the Name of Christ, forbear". A sword flashed and the defenceless monk fell to the ground. It must have been the gesture the world was waiting for. From that day to this, there have never been any more butcheries in the Colosseum in Rome.

This is a faint analogy of what happened at the Incarnation. The God we believe in is not One who sits passively on some cosmic grandstand, a detached spectator who looks on the suffering of men untouched by a feeling of our infirmities. Since He came in Christ, we know that He has descended into the arena of our struggles and cruel agonies, and has become inextricably involved in the human predicament. It is because God became involved in history that we must get involved. It is because He cared, even unto Calvary, that we too must compassionately minister to all for whom Christ has died.

Finally the Christian rejoices in the knowledge that God's purpose is invincible. At the height of the battle of Trafalgar, Nelson was mortally wounded and carried below deck. There with stoic courage, he unflinchingly endured as the Scottish surgeon probed for the embedded musket ball. As his strength ebbed and his colour faded, he was heard, again and again, asking, "How goes the battle?" When at last Hardy, the second in command, bent over him and said, "You have won a great victory", a radiant smile transformed the drawn, pain-puckered face.

There is a sense in which every Christian must be a Nelson. It does not matter what happens to us as long as the battle for righteousness, raging in the world, is won. Our own failures and successes are unimportant as long as the purpose of God is undefeated. Even when we ourselves are cruelly thwarted, we rejoice in the knowledge that there is an invincible power at the heart of things. We rejoice in the conviction that through life there runs a purpose which decrees that every Calvary has its Easter day and every winter its resurgent spring. We rejoice in the assurance that this corruptible must put on incorruption, that this mortal must put on immortality, and that what eye has not seen nor ear heard is laid up as a final consummation for those that love God. In life, sorrow is never absent, but joy is always present, and for the Christian it is the dominant note.

5

THE ONENESS OF LIFE

"For by one Spirit are we all baptised into one body."

I Corinthians 12, 13

In the twelfth chapter of his first letter to the Corinthians, Paul deals with the schismatic tendencies that had already become evident in the early Church. The other conflict which threatened to tear the Church apart was one which centred round the comparative prestige of teachers, preachers and prophets. The Apostle makes no effort to placate any of the local prejudices, nor does he pretend that ominous cracks do not exist. Unerringly he diagnoses the sectarian canker in its early stage of growth and his answer is as valid now as it was within the divisive Corinthian Church of the first century. Making no concessions to disunity, he simply wrote: "For by one Spirit are we all baptised into one body, whether we be Jews or Gentiles, whether we be bond or free."

One of the commonest ways of evading the Christian challenge is to admit it is a beautiful ideal, but that unfortunately it does not work in a world of tough and brutal actualities. But this popular escape route is based on a presupposition which will not bear close scrutiny. It is perfectly true that Christianity presents us with lofty ideals that tower above us like dizzy

Himalayan peaks, but it is equally true that it also presents us with facts as concrete and down to earth, as durable and dependable as any of the facts disclosed to us by science.

It is significant that when Paul was dealing with dissension at Corinth, he did not appeal to idealism but to a fact which no amount of clever sophistry could dissolve. He did not argue that Christians, because they acknowledge One Lord and One Saviour, ought to regard themselves as one body: he categorically asserted that they were already one body. What I want to do in this sermon then is to show that Paul's affirmation is relevant not only to the Church, but to the whole of life.

We are one body. This affirmation is true in respect of the oneness of knowledge. The Industrial Revolution launched in Britain about the middle of the eighteenth century gathered such momentum that by the beginning of the nineteenth our technical supremacy was unrivalled and unquestioned. Anyone who fondly supposes that we shared out our secrets to impoverished nations, struggling to reach a modest subsistence level, must be exceedingly naïve. We did not. On the contrary, British artisans were forbidden to seek employment on the continent, and commercial spying by foreigners was regarded as a punishable crime. In our selfishness we failed to see that any attempt to localise knowledge was as stupid as King Canute's celebrated bid to stop the tide. The fact that Britain has long since been outstripped industrially, is a humiliating reminder that, where knowledge is concerned, we are one body.

Man learns by experience, we say, but this is not always so. Individuals and communities dominated by self-interest, have a sublime capacity for shutting their eyes to all historical precedents. So in 1945 America invented the MacMahon Act to prevent the rest of the world from acquiring atomic secrets—another attempt to limit and localise knowledge, monumental in its stupidity. Within a few years, Russia, Britain and France in turn were in possession of the nuclear know-how, which was so furtively acquired and so jealously guarded—a further demonstration of the fact that where knowledge is concerned, we are one body.

In the heyday of her supremacy, the Church did not encourage freedom of scientific research. Galileo and his contemporaries were persecuted, and even Isaac Newton was savagely maligned when he formulated his law of gravitation. In retrospect it is easy to feel superior to medieval obscurantism, but the fallacy defended was essentially the same as that of the British when they were pioneers of technology, and of the Americans when they posed as Lords of the Atom. The Church mistakenly assumed that the Bible was the repository of all truth and that anyone who dared question its infallibility was guilty of blasphemy. Apparently it did not occur to them that the God of the Bible was the same God who set the planets in motion and regulated the temperature of the human body; that the God revealed by Jesus was also the author of truth in all its myriad branches and manifestations. Such a recognition on the part of the Church would have prevented the alienation of the intellectuals which now stands as a major obstacle in the path of evangelism.

In his controversial book, *The Two Cultures*, C. P. Snow pleaded for a closer understanding between scientists on the one hand and literary intellectuals on the other. This is surely a pre-eminently reasonable plea, but Christians must be prepared to go much further. They must plead for a reciprocal understanding between all branches of knowledge. On no account must they shiver in apprehension lest the astronomer and biologist, in their most recent discoveries, have brought to light something which discredits the Christian faith. They must rest secure in the conviction that God is the author of all truth and that, therefore, scientists and theologians, philosophers and literary intellectuals, have been "baptised into one body".

We are one body. Again this affirmation is true in respect of our common humanity. Our world has shrunk to an amazing degree both in space and in time. This is dramatically brought home to us by the fact that a man-made machine can orbit the earth in less than an hour and a half. But our legitimate pride in man's technical ingenuity is tempered by the recognition that his social conscience has not kept pace with his scientific achievements. Physically, the peoples of the world are neighbours, living cheek by jowl, but spiritually they can be poles apart.

Our world is divided into the haves and the have-nots, the children of affluence and the children of affliction. It is surely ironic that though Jesus stated it was hardly possible for a rich man to enter the Kingdom of Heaven, the wealthiest countries by far in the world today are the Christian ones. In Church-conscious America the average annual income five years ago was £750. In Britain it was £300. But in over one hundred under-developed countries and territories it was less than £30. Not only do we accept these cruel anomalies with a complacent conscience, but at election time the contending political parties try to cajole the masses by a naked appeal to their selfish and acquisitive instincts.

If we believe that God is our Father and that all men, whatever the colour of their skin, are our brothers, we cannot nimbly sidestep the challenge of our common humanity. We must ask ourselves whether we are prepared to forego another rise in our standard of living that millions living on the edge of famine, and millions more suffering from chronic malnutrition, might have one square meal a day. The truth is, and no self-respecting economist can deny it, that the advanced countries are not paying the under-developed ones anything like near enough for their commodities. We are waxing fat literally at the expense of hungry people.

The Paley Report, published in America in 1952, shocked the world by its revelations. It disclosed that the country we all took to be self-sufficient got over half of certain vital minerals from the backward countries. This surely puts a different complexion on things. It is becoming increasingly clear that the help the under-developed territories of the earth need must stem, not from a spurious philanthropy, nor from a "be kind to the underdog" brand of humanitarianism, but from the intelligent recognition that this is our only hope of survival.

The time has come when we must stop talking in terms of ideals, and, like Paul, begin talking in terms of facts. To improve our own standard of living at the expense of others is a suicidal policy. Such selfishness is a form of cancer, a case of certain cells growing and multiplying by feeding on others. To glory in the affluent society of the West and preach Christianity to the hungry millions who have to make do on less than £30 a year is practical atheism at its very ugliest. The moment any man confesses, "I believe in God, the Father Almighty", he must in the same breath acknowledge our common humanity, and with the Apostle affirm that we are all "baptised into one body".

We are one body. Finally this affirmation is true in respect of our salvation. Paul knew what he meant when he used the word salvation. So did Luther and Wesley and Thomas Chalmers, but this word, which used to speak so clearly and so powerfully to our fathers, today only confounds, carrying with it all sorts of incredible connotations. This is one reason why preaching is so ineffective and why the world turns a deaf ear to our pronouncements.

The word salvation has suffered devaluation because for too long we have gloried in a false individualism. We have sponsored the belief that a man is most truly himself, his honest-to-goodness, rugged self, when he stands alone, independent of all collective influences. Such a person is not possible, and if by the wildest stretch of imagination he were, he is someone very different from the new man in Christ the New Testament proclaims, not as a promise but as an actuality.

Furthermore, the word has been largely drained of its original meaning because we have come to do business with a small God who has been stripped of his cosmic stature. The conventional God, worshipped in many churches, is a displaced person in His own world. Elbowed out from the centre of things, He has retained a precarious foothold on the slippery ledge of what we call personal experience. For the majority of people, God exists for one purpose and one purpose only—to solve their individual problems and to bequeath to them the desired amount of individual happiness. Such a God is blasphemously irrelevant in the atomic age. How can we believe in a God who is able to save us from drink and sex, but is powerless before the challenge of world hunger, the sanctified evil of race prejudice, and the menace of the Bomb waiting to go off.

It is a desperately disturbing fact that on practically every important social issue the scientific humanists feel more deeply and act with a sense of greater urgency than the mass of conventional Christians. When Bertrand Russell, the aged apostle of agnosticism, despatches a strongly-worded telegram to Mr. Khrushchev pleading with him to limit the death sentence in Russia, we cannot help wondering why so many professed believers clamour for its extension in this country. They refuse to see that we are members one of another and that there is a real sense in which we are in varying degrees responsible for all that happens in our society. Christians are ready to listen to fallible judges, fallible civil servants and fallible governments, but not to the Christ who denounced violence and authoritatively declared that in God's world it is not possible for Satan to cast out Satan.

What I am really pleading for is a New Testament conception of salvation. Paul uses the metaphor of the body to drive home what he means by it. The human organism with its intricate and delicate network of nerves is so sensitive that a pain in any one part of it, in a tooth, in an eye, even in a little finger, instantaneously communicates itself to all the rest. Similarly, Christians are members one of another, so closely and so indissolubly united that the suffering of the most insignificant individual should be felt by the entire community.

But what of personal assurance, someone may reasonably interject. Is it not possible for the individual to cry out from the depth of his own experience, "O God thou art my God"? Indeed it is. There is no necessary contradiction between personal and social salvation, for there is a sense in which they are basically one. Robinson Crusoe experienced a dramatic form of conversion on the island where he was cast up without a single companion. But it would be wrong to deduce from this that he was a lone Christian wolf, demonstrating once and for all that solitary Christianity is a practical possibility. Robinson Crusoe had his Bible with him, therefore in faith he was united with the universal community, the Body of Christ revealed in the Word of God.

The word salvation is ambiguous, but we do no

violence to it if we say that it means health, wholeness, well-being. The New Testament draws no sharp distinction between body and soul such as we do, but regards man as an indivisible unity. Nor does it admit of any artificial separation between the individual and the community. The Christian religion is a relation between the individual soul and God, but it is a relation that can be realised only within the believing community. Jesus promised His Presence not to the individual in solitariness, but to the faithful community, "For where two or three are gathered together in my name, there am I in the midst of them." Salvation is meaningless without this sense of togetherness. This is the conviction Paul is so eager to convey to the divided Church in Corinth when he writes, "For by one Spirit are we all baptised into one body."

Illustrations

23 b.
33 m.
49 b the call to obey